REAL PEOPLE REVI

Jenny Neill from Connect Emotional Ed ... .u-
*ral storyteller, Adam finds joy in the mundane, stories in soft play
and humour in hypnobirthing. Each short chapter stands alone -
perfect for those days (read: everyday) when the interruptions are
constant. It's truly refreshing to hear a dad talk with such candid
honesty about his thoughts and experiences. Whilst I'm sure Adam
never set out to write a parenting manual there are threads of wis-
dom woven through the pages. Long in the tooth, been around the
block parents will smile wryly and feel seen. Those navigating the
early days will be reassured that pretty much anything goes in this
strange, new world of parenting."*

Shay O'Carroll from Pixelmax says, *"Adam offers a unique and
refreshing insight into young family life with a level of self-depreci-
ation and honestly that most of us would struggle to reveal. Adam's
familiar writing style and keen sense of humour makes this an easy,
highly enjoyable read while highlighting a loving parental bond. This
quote captures exactly that: "He's my son and I'm his dad and one
day when he's bigger I'm gonna tell him all about those feelings so
that one day, if he ever becomes a dad himself, he'll know it's okay to
be vulnerable."*

Kati Edwards from Birth You in Love says, *"Funny, warm-hearted
and entertaining. There are plenty of laugh out loud moments in
Adam's honest and no holds barred account of being a sleep-deprived,
domesticated, stay at home dad. With aspirations of home-ed and
ideals of the natural parenting lifestyle, Adam's provides the reader
with insight into the tough and hilarious bits of parenting."*

Tired dad, Phil Carr says, *"Having never read a book on parenting before, I expected to read theoretical examples of near*

impossible to implement advice which leaves you feeling incompetent as a parent. So, it was a lovely surprise to actually read this book - written in such a wonderful, digestible style. Each chapter is an entertaining, brutally honest, relatable short story about being a parent and a husband. I also now feel less guilty about using technology as a third parent. Overall, it was a very welcome, refreshing, and honest take on parenting from a Dad who clearly loves his kids. I'd recommend this to any parent who feels not good enough despite doing everything they can."

Hayley Mulliner from Fiddle Beads says, "*Absolutely hilarious!! You had me at the first few lines of the intro if I'm honest, I wanted to read more!! Its making me laugh and it's so, so relatable. Real, honest, and actually what happens to parents. Not all the pretty stuff, the real stuff, but in the most funny, endearing way to read. Bravo sir, I can't wait for the next one."*

WHY DO THEY ALWAYS SHOUT?

A DAD'S PERSPECTIVE.

ADAM GLENNON

Published by: Birthing Awareness Publishing
Fairway Meadows
Leicestershire
LE17
United Kingdom

www.birthingawareness.com | Mark@birthingawareness.com

isbn number: 978-1-9993791-0-0

To Janet

I hope this book brings
you some laughs!
Thanks for your support.

For Babe, Becca, and the Boys. There wouldn't be a
book to write without you... so thank you xxx
(And thanks for all the editing, Wife, because
there *definitely* wouldn't be a book without your
brutal input, ahem, constructive feedback.)

Love

FOREWORD FROM THE WIFE

When the man I met, who I was later to marry, told me he was embarking upon a career in writing, to say I was sceptical is an understatement.

We laugh now that, after my track record of relationships with men who were, let me think of the right word… unsuitable, I had planned that anybody new in my life would need to wear a suit to work, drive a flashy car and leave me alone for the majority of the time. What I actually got was a mature student with a dream to write and not a pot to piss in.

Our first date:
'What is it you're applying to university to study?'
'Well, mental health nursing is the route I'm on at the moment,'

Oh, OK. Not quite business suit and flashy car but professional, stable, good career prospects. I'm listening …

'Nice!'

'Actually, I've decided that I was following that route for the wrong reasons. I want to write. So I'm applying for Creative Writing. It's not about having a job at the end of it, it's about creativity and following the heart.'

Cue me drinking too much rum, topping up with wine and puking over a wall while he mopped vomit out of my hair.

But, I'm glad I took a chance on love.

I could see how driven he was. His flair for telling even the most mundane stories in a hilarious, relatable way unfolded as this man I loved began to sharpen his craft. A chance "blog" recounting the homebirth of our first son, captured its essence beautifully and the journey of documenting parenthood commenced.

Adam naturally communicates the struggles of raising smalls and I'm sure you'll relate to the tales shared in *Why Do They Always Shout?* Often, our days haven't felt light-hearted. There have been tears and despondence with sleep deprivation at the core of our family for more than 6 years now. But, Adam has managed to encapsulate our history so that, looking back on even the darkest of days, I can smile with a warm heart knowing we did our best.

And, as parents, that's all we can do.

Enjoy.

From The Wife.

AN INTRODUCTION

One day I'm going to look back at this period in my life with utter amazement. Like an old explorer flicking through pictures of themselves achieving greatness by climbing Everest or trekking through the Amazon. I'll see myself and The Wife looking battered and worn through and think, how the Jeff did we survive? Is that even us in the picture? Why are my trousers on back-to-front?

But more importantly, I'll wonder how I managed to write this book while having my hypothalamus systematically pulled apart by the actions of two sleep thieves. And I won't have the answer because time is indeed a great healer. I will have pushed the painful bits deep inside by then, telling myself repeatedly that it wasn't that bad. But I'll have this book. This is the evidence which proves and documents that it did happen! That The Wife and I fought the good fight! We stared into the abyss of sleep deprived psychosis and lived to tell the tale.

You might assess from those opening words that this book is going to be a downer. That you're about to read about yet another parent moaning about their life and kids. You're not. Don't worry. I write, in the most part, something called creative non-fiction. I take moments from life with my family and invite you to live it with me in a visual, and sometimes surreal way. You may relate to these moments and find solace in the fact you're not alone. And that it's okay to feel a little bit crazy! And importantly, see the humour in it all.

Most chapters are short. A quick blast to the senses so not to over-load the reader (I know how tired you must be) with an abundance of words or details. Some topics, like lack of sleep, or using tech-nology as a third parent, may reoccur. Many issues we face as par-ents do seem to fade away and then return to us again. Sometimes slightly more challenging than before. Just when you think you have something figured out you realise you haven't. I totally get that now. I'm at peace with admitting this parenting job is the most unpredictable I've ever had.

The chapters are not presented in chronological order. This is not designed to confuse you. It's so you can flick through the book, read a few chapters, have a laugh, put the book down then pick it up again at your own leisure; possibly while hiding from your kids pretending to have a poo? Or with your back to their bedroom door during the bedtime routine maybe? It's here for you whenever you need a break in your day. With order in mind, I probably con-tradict myself occasionally. If I wrote something three years ago, warts and all; appeared to have put that issue to rest, then later be seen wrestling with the same problem again, it's probably because I forgot about it. You think you've got something figured out then wallop! Here it comes again, and you feel like a parenting rookie. If you're like us and welcomed an *unexpected* baby into your clan (see **No More Babies**) you might have discovered that none of the techniques you used first time around work the next time, so you return to a trial-and-error type of parenting style which can be tough going with mixed results.

We get it!

There's a mixture of writing styles that hopefully keep you enter-tained and snippets of **Flash Non-Fiction**. You won't have many names to remember either. There's The Wife, Claire. Stepdaughter, Becca (look out for her in **Conversations with a Teenager**) and Arlo and Ove, the stars of the show, our little sleep thieves, who at the time of writing this introduction are 5 and 3 years old. They are the greatest source of inspiration who take me to the very edge of sanity in one breath then transport me to the fluffiest inner depths of love the next.

We share a lot of laughs in life which often sit alongside an array of emotions and learning opportunities - most I feel ill-equipped to understand because I'm just so tired. So very tired. Hungover at least twice a week as well of course but we all need a little treat don't we? Treats comes in different shapes and sizes but for me personally, alcohol is usually my go-to choice and I'm honest (several **A Lockdown Story** chapters explore this) about what happened to me when the treats replaced the healthier habits in my life; how this effected my ability to parent, and how I pulled myself out of it and returned to wellness.

Sometimes this parenting malarkey feels like treading water though doesn't it? Waiting for a lifeline to be thrown in that never really comes. You realise treading water's getting you nowhere, so you get motivated, raise your head and start swimming and if you have one, your partner appears on the horizon in a boat made from hope, looking strong and smiley, with the kids secured inside a large net. They drop you off somewhere warm and quiet, while you recuperate then sometime later you return the favour when you see your co-parent struggling for breath.

It's hard work. I honestly couldn't do it alone, or imagine it anyway, and I salute you amazing single parents that are.

Now I'm officially an adult, I'm able to talk about my feelings a little better than before. Pre-kids if someone had asked me, "How you feeling?" My reply would probably have been, "Alright." Whether I was or not. But now I'm well prepared to face those big feelings, and fears, head on and through **Being Dad** I'm able express myself with more confidence. I write those chapters in third person which I suppose distances myself from the content a wee bit, but that wasn't my intent. It was just a creative device to add some variety to the work.

Teamwork. Communication. Emotional intuition. All the things I forget to utilise after a prolonged period of our little sleep thieves doing what they do best, destroying our rational minds and testing our resolve. If there was a business hiring them out to someone seeking the most efficient way to induce madness, I'd be rich! I guarantee Five Star Reviews. They've pushed The Wife and I to the very limit of human endurance. It's been flipping hard work. But as we've learnt about their needs, eventually discovering that they have autism (why didn't we see this earlier?) with very individual needs, our ability to endure and adapt has expanded. This new knowledge helped to bring in some extra tolerance and patience and the realisation, whatever normal is, we don't have it. And that's fine but good to know.

We've had to dig deep. Very deep. We continue to do so. And it's completely worth it because being a parent is amazing. Mostly! Best job I've ever had. Hopefully, you feel the same. Now sit back, grab yourself a drink, get rid of those little bundles of joy for half an hour, and enjoy.

Go on, be a rebel, read in no particular order:

- ✓ Homebirth… Seriously?
- ✓ Conversations with a Teenager.
- ✓ The Bribery Trap.
- ✓ Mucky Magnificence.
- ✓ Conversations with a Kid.
- ✓ No More Babies.
- ✓ Conversations with the Wife.
- ✓ Flash Non-Fiction.
- ✓ Evolve or Medicate.
- ✓ Going Mainstream.
- ✓ Bonding without Boobs.
- ✓ Being Dad.
- ✓ Nipples with Purpose.
- ✓ The Toddler and the Telly.
- ✓ Co-sleeping with Two.
- ✓ Conversations with a Teenager.
- ✓ A Lockdown Story.
- ✓ Surviving the Summer.
- ✓ When the World made Sense.
- ✓ The Snip.
- ✓ A Lockdown Story.
- ✓ Flash Non-Fiction
- ✓ Dirty Talk.
- ✓ Being Dad.
- ✓ The Sperm Collector.
- ✓ Conversations with the Wife.
- ✓ A Force of Nature.
- ✓ For Grapes Sake.
- ✓ Meltdown Timetable.
- ✓ A Lockdown Story.
- ✓ Moving House.
- ✓ Nights Out and City Breaks.
- ✓ Be Careful.
- ✓ Flash Non-Fiction
- ✓ Living with Type 1 Diabetes.
- ✓ Conversations with a Teenager.
- ✓ A Lockdown Story.
- ✓ The Cycle of No.
- ✓ Baby Wearing's Cool.
- ✓ Conversations with the Wife.
- ✓ Talking to Strangers.
- ✓ Fuck off, Glue Ear.
- ✓ Why Do They Always Shout?
- ✓ A Lockdown Story.
- ✓ Becca.
- ✓ Jack and the Beanstalk.
- ✓ A Lockdown Story.
- ✓ They Win.
- ✓ Being Dad.
- ✓ Mums of the World… I get it Now!
- ✓ A Letter to my Boys.

HOMEBIRTH...
SERIOUSLY?

'Let me get this straight,' I say.
'You want to have the baby at home?'
'Yes.' The Wife replies.

Seven months pregnant and suddenly we've been transported back to the 1930s.

'In a, what did you call it, a birthing pool?'
'Mmmhmm.'
'A paddling pool?'
'It's not a paddling pool.'

She thrusts her phone into my face. There's a large inflatable paddling pool with *Birthing Pool* written on the side. I can tell she's geared up for this. Probably been preparing for weeks. This is not a discussion; this is an ambush. I gotta play it cool.

'But what about the mess? The baby could get stuck. What happens if you die babe? Why do you want to die?'

Okay, not cool. I'm not 100% sure what that expression on her face means but I'm pretty sure she thinks I'm an idiot. Bit harsh. My mind is being bombarded with hundreds of images of homebirth scenes from films. They all involve blood! Bloody rags, boiling water and lots of screaming. And, for reasons I can't explain, there's an elderly Irish woman in a cardigan making cups of tea and shoving me towards the door before thrusting a bottle of whiskey into my hand and telling me to "Feck off."

Not once in seven months of pregnancy has she mentioned homebirth. I consider myself an alternative thinker. I disbelieve everything the government says. Mainstream media's a joke. There's no desire from the pharmaceutical industry to cure diseases. Mars Bars are smaller. Artificial sweetener has ruined every fizzy drink and I most definitely believe in aliens. And yet having our baby at home, using a birthing pool, is the most preposterous thing I've ever heard in my life. And that's coming from someone who has never said the word *preposterous* out loud before and hopefully never will again!

'Think about every film you've ever seen, Babe. No woman survives a homebirth.'
'That's just patriarchy.'
'Ay?'
'The curse of Eve.'
'Ay?'
'Birthing is not a medical procedure. It's a natural event.'
'Okay.'
'In your head, all you can see is me screaming, enduring hours of pain surrounded by blood-soaked towels.'
'Exactly.'
'That's your conditioning.'
'Ay?'
'Statistically, you're less likely to have any complications birthing at home.'
'I'm gonna research this hippy nonsense.'

I grab my super slow laptop and switch it on. As it begins its clink-ing and humming routine, some insights begin seeping into my consciousness.

Hospitals are not fun.
Hospitals are for the sick.
Nobody likes hospitals.
Hospitals smell like they're hiding something.
Our house is nice.
It's home.
There's wine and cake here.
I know the piss on the toilet seat is mine.
We have Netflix.
Fifteen minutes later…
Homebirth makes perfect sense. Why has no one thought of this before?

'We'll have control over everything,' I say.
'Yes.'
'We could devise a relaxing playlist. Organise some mood lighting. Smelly things to create an inviting environment. Tasty treats. Maybe even a glass of organic ale?'
'And only the right people would be present. And the option of a waterbirth would be practically guaranteed.'
'But what happens if something goes wrong, Babe, seriously?'

The Wife wraps an arm around my neck and kisses me softly on the cheek.

'This is a lot to take in. Let's have a break,' she says. 'What do you want to do?'
'Erm, sex?'
'No.'
'Pub?'
'No'
'Breaking Bad?'

'Good husband.'

I turn off the laptop and get comfy on the settee, ready for a *Breaking Bad* marathon.

'And I want us to do a Hypno-Birthing course.'
'Ay? What the flip is hypno-birthing?'
'You'll like it. It's about visualisation. Breathing. Releasing a woman's natural force. We're doing it.'

I turn the laptop back on.

CONVERSATIONS WITH A TEENAGER

'You said you were gonna clean the bathroom at the weekend.'

She looks through me.

'I will.'
'Last weekend.'
'I will.'
'You will what?'
'I'll clean the bathroom.'
'You were supposed to clean it last weekend. As in, the previous one.'
'I don't know what day it is.'
'You don't know what day... a... you know what, I believe you.'
'About what?'
'That you don't know what day it is.'
'I do.'
'You just said... you win.'
'What?'
'I'll clean the bathroom myself. It's like trying to interview David Blaine for a job.'
'Who's David Blaine?'

'A famous street magician from the 90's.'

'I wasn't born then.'

'So?'

'So what?'

'For fu.. sa.. why does that mean you don't know him? You know who Jesus is?'

'Yeah.'

'And he's pretty famous, yeah?'

'Were you alive when Jesus was doing his thing?'

'No.'

'But you know who he is?'

'Yeah, but why does David Blaine want to clean our bathroom?'

'I'm going to bed.'

THE BRIBERY TRAP

Fatherhood has changed me. No doubt about it. I'm like a proper grownup. I think differently. I make sensible, well thought out decisions. I've become more empathic. Compassionate – I feeeel more. I've discovered if I share my thoughts with The Wife she won't laugh in my face and call me a wuss. In fact, most of the time I find our concerns are in alignment with each other. Which is reassuring. I dare to go a little further and suggest most of the other parents I meet in the world also share many of our worries or feelings of inadequacy. It's comforting to look around the carnage of a soft play area and know we are all just doing the best we can.

Yes, fatherhood has pushed me to grow while equally depleting me of the last dregs of youth from my face. The wrinkles are juicy and numerous around my eyes. I have the thickest grey hairs imaginable poking out of my nose and bunching together inside my ear canals. My mind is often foggy and the days blur. I dig deep to find that extra energy to play Ninjas one more time before bed but miraculously always find the strength to open a bottle of red wine once the little bundles of chubbiness have gone to sleep.

Being a stay-at-home dad has also taught me some vital practical lessons as well. Always have wipes, food, a book or toy, and a change of clothes in the bag. Basic stuff that can come in handy when faced with an unexpected dog shit disaster or an overly long wait in a queue. Actively listen to little ones, talk to them in a way in which you'd like to be spoken too. Don't match their shouts with yours and it helps to get down to their physical level when offering comfort or delivering bad news, such as, "It's time to leave soft play."

It's better to become an expert negotiator and not resort to bribery. Erm, when you figure that out, please let me know because I'm terrible at it. I never realised how intertwined bribery was with parenting. I like to kid myself it's just bargaining power but I'm fooling no one. I can't seem to get things done without offering a sweetener at the end.

"Yes, you can have a second chocolate bar, just as long as we can leave the park now."
"Yes, you can watch another episode of Paw Patrol, just as long as you understand this is the last one."

When Arlo was a toddler, I could make everything sound amazing.

"Come on, Son, leeeeets get dreeessed!"

But he figured it out. Why should he have to stop having fun with his new friends without a fuss when he can get something out of it? Now, everything's a battle. Made even more difficult now we have his wild brother to contend with. And Ove, he's a whole other level. Bribery doesn't work on children who look down at your feeble efforts. He takes great pleasure from doing the complete opposite of what you ask and that's enough pleasure for him. Stuff ya chocolate.

In a previous life I would scoff into my single man's red wine, watching parents shove iPhones into their kids' faces in restaurants. "You'll never see me do that," scoff, scoff, scoff. Parents pleading with their kids to simply sit still for five minutes while they finished their Buffalo Wings. "You need to put your foot down, mate," scoff, scoff, scoff.

What a fool. What a naïve fool I was. I really miss that guy.

How did I fall into this trap? Sleep deprivation probably. Wanting an easy life, definitely. But it's not an easy life is it? Not in the end. Eventually, I'll have nothing to give, and then what? When they've tasted all the cakes, watched all the DVD's and drunk all the variations of nonconcentrated organic juice this world has to offer, what's next? I have this vision of Arlo walking into the kitchen while I'm slaving over the stove, watching as he grabs one of my German Beers from the fridge and using the spur on Woody's boot to flick the top off before taking a long gulp.

'What you doing with my beer, Son?'
'Your beer? Get on with tea Old Man.'

I think I've figured it out though. I've been trying to protect him from feelings of disappointment. When he reacts to a decision which infringes upon his happiness, like leaving a fun event or not eating all the grapes in one sitting - I've plastered over his natural response to disappointment with a reward system that only delays his frustration before it moves onto the next issue. And it's because it hurts me to see him in pain. More so when I'm the cause of it.

This cannot continue.

The solution. Better time management. Example: We need to be somewhere for 10 am, begin the process of getting ready the night before. Leaves plenty of time for leeway. Simpler days – less activities. Rather than try and do shopping in the morning, park mid-morning, and library after lunch, just focus on one activity without an agenda. This leaves plenty of space for more spontaneous interactions. Finally, my boys are going to get frustrated. Tired. Annoyed. But I think that's only a small percentage of the day compared to the rest which is filled with laughter and fun.

Seriously, I'm like a proper grownup now. Scary.

MUCKY MAGNIFICENCE

Arlo makes friends wherever we go. Even older children who look at him like he's some crazy-talking-fictional-character at first, warm to him eventually. He's relentless in his eagerness to have fun and that's infectious. This puts me in contact with a lot of new faces. You could label some cute. Others, energised. "Spirited," a Gran might say. But the majority can only be described as mucky! Existing on some level between disgusting and icky. It's not their clothes, which are usually pretty mucky too, (you can tell they were clean when they put them on in the morning) it's more of an aura of muckiness. Smears of snot like snail trails glistening from certain angles on the side of their faces. Sticky warm hands covered in hidden germs and everything else they've touched in the last hour. Including, and in no particular order: Their bum hole, genitals, the bit of the toilet no adult would touch without rubber gloves, something that was originally solid but has softened in their warm clammy grip, fluff and dust off a floor which has become intertwined with the stickiness of their being.

I include my boy Ove in this. 100%. He looks mucky after a bath. That's not easy to achieve, so I'm sympathetic to the plight of the *mucky child phenomena* which is a blight in any parent's day.

But I recently witnessed something so unbelievable it's difficult to describe its mucky-magnificence. Arlo was playing with a boy at soft play. They'd been running wild around the place while me and Ove had a leisurely stroll from area to area without agenda. This boy's face was always out of view. I thought nothing of it at first but then the first tingles of awareness sparkled and snapped around at my consciousness. An ancient, reptilian part of my brain was alerted - *protect your child, there's muckiness afoot.* I grabbed Ove and slid him into his sling. Together we approached the mouth of the large climbing, slidey, ball pit area where only the brave will enter. Ove looked at me with his pure blue knowing eyes.

'Yes, Son. We must go in.'

He pointed towards the flashy arcade game in the corner and mumbled.

'No. Arlo needs us.'

I tightened the sling around us. I wasn't going to lose this one. We entered. I pushed through the long lightweight punch bags hanging from metal bars. A toddler was in the corner headbutting the fence while crying. I asked him if he needed help. He stopped headbutting the fence and began laughing hysterically. We left him to it. Arlo and his friend stomped above us and ran across a rickety bridge. I only glimpsed the bottom of their socks but I knew it was them. We took a left and began climbing up a strappy thing to the next level where we came face-to-face with what can only be described as the lost children from Mad Max. They'd been long forgotten by their carers, parents, whoever it was who'd brought them to this place. I tried to pass them without being seen but it was hopeless.

'Mama?' asked a child wearing a potato sack for a dress.

I didn't make eye contact and she wandered towards an inflated tube with a clown face.

'Mama?' she repeated.

I placed my back against the sponge wall and moved along a corridor towards the entrance to the next level, but the Mad Max children had sensed my presence.

'Dadda?' a boy with half a haircut asked.

I shook my head and shushed him, but it was too late. The docile pack had been awakened. They'd never seen a man under sixty years old on a workday and they wanted one badly. Kids dropped from the padded scaffold all around us. Others dragged themselves over brightly coloured patched up barriers. Their eyes were wild with excitement. Ove squeezed my shoulder.

'I know, Son. I love you.'

We pushed forward.

'Daddy?'

I guided that boy down the slide to my left.

'Dadda?'

Sorry little Princess. I point to the floor.

'Look.'

Several of them including a haggard looking Snow White look down and I pressed on.

The children parted and a little girl, the leader I think, made her way to the front of the pack. Smaller children hissed at her, but she scolded them with a look, and they recoiled into the shadows. She turned her attention back to me.

'My Daddy,' she said.

The pack began slapping the floor and stamping their feet like demented chimps as they approached us. We were done for. But suddenly, from out of the darkness to our left, flickers of light began to sting the children's eyes as dangly strips of fabric were disturbed by a chubby fist. I took the opportunity and jumped onto a separate platform as a truly mucky toddler wobbled his way into the centre of the pack. He looked around. Unwittingly. Not sensing any danger. Innocent. He held out a hand which clutched a white semi-chewed ball of deconstructed toast.

'Toast?' he exclaimed.

He never stood a chance. The pack completely forgot I existed and homed in on that poor boy. He looked towards me, confused at first then angry, as the pack began clawing at the prize in his grip. This gave us the vital seconds required to scramble to safety. I looked over my shoulder one last time as a Peppa Pig and Paw Patrol enthusiast pushed him to the floor while the pack surrounded him.

'Thank you,' I whispered. 'Your sacrifice will not be in vain.'

The higher we climbed the hotter it got. Greece, in the height of summer, hot. I thought somebody was cooking kebabs in the ball pit, but it was the smell from my armpits which was oozing toxins stored from Creamfields Festival 1999. Some fresh- faced kids appeared waving small balls in the air and smiling. They were using gestures and a dialect I couldn't understand. I dodged, nudged and continued to climb until coming face-to-face, sort of, with Arlo and the back of his new friend's head. All noise was sucked from the room as if a great sound collecting vacuum had been switched on. It darkened. A chill filled the air and the damp patches under my arms and across my chest froze instantly. Ove looked at me. I nodded. We'd come this far. The only way back down was on the multi-coloured slide less than five metres away. We scrambled onto the final platform where Arlo and his friend were sitting.

'Hi, Daddy,' Arlo shouted.

His new friend turned suddenly before I could reply. Ove grasped my hand. The illuminous snot hanging from this kid's nose was nothing short of miraculous. I was hypnotised by its shear other-worldliness. I wanted to prod it with a stick but I had no stick. No sense of space or time. Was it real? Is anything real?

This living organism attached to that child's face made me question my very existence. But I acted swiftly.

'You need to go find your mum, or whoever you're with, sharpish and ask them to wipe your nose, mate.'

He knew. His eyes told me so. I respected him at that moment. He had the presence of mind to not wipe *it* on his thin sleeve - he would've needed an arm longer than an orangutan to achieve this anyway. Instead he chose to continue enjoying himself. Allowing *it* to exist on his face. Neither boy concerned about any social faux pas, such as spinach in the teeth or in this case, a new organ developing on his philtrum. But unlike these children, I have a keen eye for such things, so I pointed with a finger and nudged him with a toe towards the slide.

'Go on – go, get, go on.'

He rolled away and slid down the bumpy slide headfirst on his back, never breaking eye contact with me for a moment. Neither did *it*. I tried to take my eyes away, but it was simply too amazing. He disappeared from view. I removed Ove from the sling and we both hugged Arlo, who had no idea he'd been in the presence of a medical marvel.

'Shall we go down the slide, boys?'

'Yeah,' they agreed.

We took up positions at the top of the slide. I turned to my right.

'Are you ready, Arlo?'

He was. I turned to the left.

'Ove?'

He was ready too. I turned back to Arlo and his friend had returned with a handful of Cadburys Buttons melting in his grasp. Chocolate smeared all over his now snot-less face. I pointed to the ceiling, creating a moments distraction, then pushed both my boys down the slide to safety.

We never looked back.

CONVERSATIONS
WITH A KID

'I think I want to marry a boy and a girl when I'm older.'
'Covering your bases. Good idea, Son.'
'But I'll wait until I'm much older.'
'Sounds sensible.'
'You'll be dead then.'
'Cheers, Son.'

'How old are you, Dad?'
'39.'
'That's really old.'
'Er, it's not that old actually.'
'You're going to die soon.'
'Cheers, Son.'

'Hi, Dad.'
'Hello, Son.'
'Did you have a good day at work?'
'It was alright. Nothing special.'
'Maybe you should get another job?'
'When you're a bit older maybe.'
'You'll be dead then.'
'Cheers, Son.'

NO MORE BABIES

'So that's it, no more babies?' The Wife says.

I hold her hand, look lovingly into her eyes.

'I'd prefer to put my balls in a blender than go through this again.'
'Don't say that! Arlo's amazing.'
'He is. But could we really survive having another baby that sleeps like him? I don't even want to think about it.'

She's gutted. I know she's stuck between wanting me to say, "Yeah, let's do it, Babe. Let's see how much sleep deprivation two humans can endure. Let's think of it as a science project.' And "No, piss off."

Piss off seems much easier than the other option right now.

'Right, well you'd better go and get the snip then cos I'm not going back on the pill.'
'Don't you think that's a bit drastic?'
'Why's it always got to be on the woman?'

Of course, I have a minor responsibility in all of this.

'How about the withdrawal method,' I offer. Jokingly.

She ain't laughing. Got to turn this around quickly.

'Aren't there some natural ways? I'm sure I read something about temperature control. Plus you haven't had a period for ages now. The way that boy keeps draining your boobs we'll be right for a while yet.'
'Not really a long-term option is it?'
'No. I guess not. We could get some condoms from the family planning place. Ribbed for your pleasure.'

She looks at me like I'm the biggest idiot she's ever met in her life, with a, *how did I ever let you impregnate me* kind of expression. I need to take this seriously.

'Babe, are you sad because you won't get to have a little baby again? Is that what it is?'

I've knocked the nail right on the head and The Wife's eyes fill with tears.

'Listen, why don't we get some condoms for a bit. Mix it up with a spot of mutual masturbation and see how we feel in a year or so? You never know, Arlo might be sleeping through by then and we'll be in the right mental state to talk about it properly.'

She wipes her snotty nose.

'So it's not completely off the table?'
'Nothing's ever completely off the table, Babe.'

Balls in a blender! I totally mean it.

'Come here.'

We have a *nice* long hug, which turns into a *nice* slow kiss, then right on cue, my beautiful little cock blocker Arlo wakes up screaming from an afternoon nap in his bedroom and we both go and see to him.

'Little boy, Mummy's here, it's okay.'

He calms down and attaches himself to his favourite thing in the world, The Wife's boob.

'We need a night out. I'm gonna ask my mum to come and have him for an evening.'
'But she won't be able to put him to bed.'
'If we don't let her give it ago we'll never know will we? Let's ask her to come early evening, we'll go for a meal, smash a bottle of red, eat, smoke a cig then come home to deal with it.

What do you reckon?'

I watch her mind complete a full risk assessment.

'Sounds great, let's do it.'
'Yes!'

The following week - I think. Could have been a year, another life, the next day, sleep deprivation is no joke, Granny arrives to look after Becca and Arlo for a few hours.

'Cheers, Mum. We'll be back for 7ish.'
'Don't worry, we'll be fine,' Granny says.

I know The Wife wants to explain in great detail what we have already written down on a piece of paper and given to Granny, but I pull her by the arm towards the gate. This is the first time we've both been separated from Arlo since his birth nearly nineteen months ago. And he is not happy about it.

'He'll be fine when you've gone, don't worry, just go.'

The Wife's body is like a rock. All of her motherly instincts are screaming in her head, "He needs you, he needs you," and I'm sure Arlo feels the same but we need this. We deserve this.

'Come on, Babe."

My voice breaks the spell and she's allowed to be guided down the path away from the house. It's horrible. Is it supposed to be this hard? The Wife's crying. I'm thirsty. We can still hear Arlo screaming. Then suddenly, it stops. The door has been shut and I make sure The Wife moves in the direction of the Italian restaurant where we have a reservation for an early bird deal.

Five minutes later:
'Shall I call to see if he's okay?'
'No.'
Twelve minutes later:
'I'm just gonna call to see-'
'No.'

Fifteen minutes later at the restaurant ordering wine and food:

'Do you think he's alright?'
'Probably.'
'Why probably?'
'Because I don't know. I can guarantee he's not been left to play with the knives.'
'Why would you say that?'
'Because I trust my mum to take care of him.'
'I'm calling.'
'NO.'

Twenty-three minutes later:

'This wine is nice.'
'My boobs are leaking.'

Twenty-five minutes later:

'I just called your mum when I was in the toilet sorting my boob out. He's fine. They're watching Lion King.'
'See. Now you can chill out a bit.'

Forty Minutes Later:

My phone rings.

'Is that your mum? Is he okay?'
'I'm just trying to get it out of my pocket.'
'I knew it. Get the bill.'

She stands up.

'It's Becca. Sit down, Babe.'

She reluctantly perches back on the edge of her seat.

'Hi, what's up?'

The Wife is burning a hole through my head with her heat vision eyes!

'In the top draw in our bedroom. Yes. We're having a nice time. We'll see you in an hour or so.'

I turn the phone off and place it on the table.

'Spare diddy.'

She lets out a sigh of relief so heavy, heads turn and glasses rattle on their tables.

We made it through the rest of the evening without interruption. The Wife's trying to act cool, like she's not removing my arm from the socket as she pulls me up the street towards our house. I hope that noise I can hear is something other than her grinding her teeth otherwise they're going to be chalk dust by the time we get in.

'Are you okay, Babe?'
'Mm mm.'

Her expression softens and the grinding ends as we arrive at the front door. No screaming baby. The house isn't a pile of burning rubble after all. Nor has a pack of baby eating wolves escaped from the zoo and figured out where we keep the spare key. I smile and touch her face gently.

'We made it. Our first night-'
'Keys.'
'Ay?'
'Get the keys out of your pocket and open the door.'
'Oh yeah.'

The hallway light sparks to life and The Teenager opens the front door.

'Hi, Mum.'
'Hey. It's very quiet in there.'
'He's in bed,' Granny says from the shadows of the kitchen.
'No way,' we both say simultaneously.
'I told you it'd be alright.'

She looks like she's aged ten years. Plus, I never noticed she had a twitch before. I can already see the gin and tonic she'll be leathering when she gets home.

'You did. I don't know why I was so worried, thanks,' The Wife says.
'Any time,' Granny says. 'Just not for the next couple of weeks because we're going to Portugal.'

Pretty sure she booked that holiday this evening using her phone.

'That sounds lovely. Thanks again,' The Wife says as she barges past Becca and Granny and disappears up the stairs.

I turn to give my mum a kiss but she's already running at full speed up the path. Her coat's flailing behind her like Batman's cape because of the G-force created by the speed she's generating.

'See you, Mum.'

The last thing I see is the soles of her shoes as she dives headfirst over the seven-foot bush at the front of the garden.

'How was it?' I ask Becca.
'I don't think we'll be seeing her for a while.'
'At least we had tonight. You okay?'
'I'm going bed. You might not see me for a while either.'
'Haha. Good night.'

After tidying up downstairs a little, I open a bottle of red and pour two glasses. The Wife appears wearing a dressing gown.

'He's flat out,' she says.
'Amazing. Now if we could just figure out why he won't do that for us, that'd be fantastic.'

She comes over to me and starts touching my ear.

'What you doing? Why you wearing a dressing gown? It's like eight o'clock.'
'Thought we'd go upstairs for a bit of, you know?'
'I've just opened the wine.'

She leans forward and gives me a nice kiss – extra tongue.

'Wine's for losers,' I say as I'm led away from the kitchen up the stairs.

Less than ten minutes later:

We both stare up at the ceiling. The lovemaking sweat has already been replaced with a cold panicky one. We both feel it. We look into each other's eyes. This is one of those moments when only a single word can describe a feeling.

'Shit.'

Nine months later… you know the rest!

CONVERSATIONS WITH THE WIFE

I know what she wants.

She thinks she's so clever.

But she's not. Not even a little bit.

'You haven't worn that jumper for ages, it looks great,' she says.

I throw her a half-smile from my end of the sofa.

'Fanks.'

I return to *Outlander,* which she knows I've been waiting to read for ages; just needed to be in the right mood, and have no kids doing my head in. And I'm in that right mood!

'You look goood.'

That was embarrassing.

I nod my head.

Turn a page.

'I didn't know you'd been working out.'

Does she really believe I'm that gullible?

'I haven't.'
'Seriously? Wow. Your arms look huge.'
'I don't want huge arms.'

I remain focused on the book in my hand. I can tell that just threw her off. Big time.

'Erm… not huge exactly. Shapely.'

Ha ha. Nice try. Now piss off.

'Hmm mm.'

I push myself a little further into the sofa, clearly showing my intention to stay right here in this spot, reading my book, chilling out, living these precious childless moments in peace.

Shit.

She's good. Flipping good! In one silky movement she raised her feet off the floor, tucked them under my bum slightly, creating the illusion of needing warmth and comfort. In reality, it's to give me a not-so-gentle shove in the direction of the kitchen.

Sometimes I forget who I'm dealing with. The manipulative skills. The planning.

'My feet are freezing but you're so waaaaarrrrm.'

There must be a way to fight back!

'Put the heating on if you like?'

She was not expecting that.

'What? During the day?'
'Yeah, why not. Go for it.'

Having the heating on during the day is a rare occasion. You literally need to have snot icicles hanging from your blue nose before it's turned on. And here I am offering it up on a plate. I glance over at her. She's proper torn. She can't just ask me to get up and turn it on. No, no, that would spoil the game. It must appear to be of my own choosing, you see. That's the game. On the other hand, she could just get up and sort it herself... but she won't.

'Why? Do you want to turn it on?' she asks.

Do you see what she did there?

'I'm fine. I have my muscly jumper on.'
'I don't want to put the heating on... just for me.'

Bloody evil genius.

Two can play that game Bobby Brown!

My eyes remain fixed on *Outlander* as I reach behind the sofa, like any thoughtful husband would, and grab her a blanket.

'There you go, Bobby.'
'Ay?'
'Nothing.'
'Okay. Thanks.'

A minute later.

Her feet are now making me really uncomfortable. Her sharp nails are practically slicing my spinal cord as she wriggles her feet against my lower back under the guise of generating warmth.

I smile at her.

She smiles back.

Wriggle, wriggle, slice, slice. Go on, slice away, I hope you sever it! You'll have to get a new slave then and I'll be able to read my book in peace. Just hurry up about it, cos you're doing my head in! I reckon her toes must be aching by now. She's willing to sacrifice her own comfort just to force me off the sofa and into the kitchen, but I won't give in. Not today.

'So comfy,' she lies.
'Hmm mm.'
'Did you buy any biscuits yesterday?'

She's already scoffed half the packet.

'Hmm mm.'
'Which ones.'
'Rich Tea.'
'Perfect to dunk in a brew.'

THERE! SHE FINALLY SAYS THE WORDS OUT LOUD! THE FAÇADE IS OVER!

'If you say so.'

Now she's smacking her lips together to indicate her mouth is dry.

'Cough, cough.'

She's piling it on.

We're entering the endgame now.

'Are you thirsty, Babe?' I ask.
'Yeah, I'd love a…'
'Here.'

I look into her eyes. Her lovely face. I smile and slowly reach towards the side of the sofa; her eyes follow the movement of my hand. She knows what's coming and I know she knows because I sense the pained disappointment in her soul.

'Here you go.'

I pass her a bottle of water.

Not today, Wife!

'Fanks,' she says.

Ha. Victory. Nowhere left to go. Game – set – match.

'Is that your phone ringing?'

Shit. It's in the kitchen.

'It's fine.'
'It could be important.'
'I don't get important calls.'
'It could be school or nursery?'
'It won't be.'
'You don't know that.'
'I do.'
'Answer the phone.'
'No.'
'Why you being weird?'
'I'm not.'
'You are.'

'I just want to read Outlander in peace.'
'You can. Just answer the phone first.'
'Right.'

Her aching toes give it one last hurrah and kindly help me up off the sofa. She's flipping beaming. Radiating. I turn away so she can't see every fibre of my being oozing with disappointment and defeat. My face cannot lie. I arrive at the kitchen just as the phone stops ringing.

'Who was it?'
'Shitty private number.'
'That's annoying.'

Three, two, one.

'Stick the kettle on, Babe.'

Evil genius!

FLASH NON-FICTION

I open my eyes.

The bedroom is quiet.

No kids. It's morning.

What the flip is going on?

The Wife's still sleeping.

She looks peaceful.

My mouth isn't dry.

It's light outside. Birds are singing.

No kids in the bed.

I can't remember the last time… hang on.

Why am I Robbie Williams?

The Wife holds my wrist.

She's the receptionist from my dentist.

'Are you okay?' The Receptionist asks.

I nod my head and smile.

Her grip tightens.

'They are coming,' she hisses.

I open my eyes.

It's dark. Cold.

Neither day nor night.

Two loud thuds from the other bedroom disturbs the silence.

I turn to The Wife.

Her eyes are open wide.

She pulls a pillow tight into her chest.

'They are here!'

EVOLVE OR MEDICATE.

I'm turning into a massive softy. And I don't mean my midriff, which already resembles a pack of jam swiss rolls, I'm talking about my inner workings – those things I've avoided since childhood. You know what I mean, my emo… ahem. Those fee… ahem. You know, don't make me say it! Okay. Here we go. *I'm becoming more in-tune with my emotions. I have deeper feelings about my life and family.* There, I said it. Life used to be so simple. Now there's all this extra stuff to think about. It's very unsettling.

Did I ever imagine parenting would have this effect on me? Not at all. Was I naïve? Absolutely! Do I blame the kids for making me look inside and consider the notion of personal growth? A resounding yes!

It's my own fault really. I could have been one of those full-time working dads who get an hour or two in the evening then cram it all into the weekend. Not me. I wanted to be present. I wanted to be there during these early years because The Wife assured me it was the most important time in a child's development. In our relationship. When I was a kid, no one ever used phrases like *development*. You were dragged up and on Fridays you got a Twix and a can of pop. On super special occasions you got a chippy tea, and you were bloody grateful for it. Especially if you got a white barmcake as well (some of you might not know what a barmcake is and that's okay.) Now there's all these phrases and buzz words which make it difficult to navigate this tricky world of parenting. The possibility of feeling guilty is there at every turn. I wasn't even fully aware of what guilt felt like before becoming a parent. Blissful ignorance was a preferred state of being. Not anymore. Now I know. And so I've learnt, with regret, that when you feel that guilt, stuffing your kids with chocolate, a chippy tea, buying them toys or any type of material grand gesture isn't the way to solve the issue.

Who knew?

I spend a lot of time with my boys. The Wife is career orientated where I'm more domesticated. I love nothing more than noticing the right kind of light breeze, combined with just enough sunshine, then getting the washing on the line. Makes my day that. I appear to be the only human in our house capable of picking clothes up off the floor or emptying the recycling. And if I didn't prepare the meals, they'd all have scurvy by now. There's not much time for anything else. Having a parent stay home brings financial hardship. One income isn't enough to thrive exactly. But as someone who has been in and out of Adult Education, I've learnt to stretch the shopping money further by making tough choices. Two-ply toilet paper is just enough, as long as your fingers don't go through that is. Bit of trial and error with that one. Home baking, batch cooking, boxes of wine, stuff like that.

Budgeting is a skill.

Being at home has boosted my tolerance levels because there's a definite tendency to want to scream more than normal when you're with your kids, day in, day out. I get it, they're my kids. Of course, it's my responsibility to care for them, who else would do that better? But it's not like I have extensive parenting knowledge. One day I was a solitary beast then the next I'm part of a pack. A very strange pack. No one at work has ever wiped their shit on my trousers while I wasn't looking or screamed in my face for cutting a sandwich at the wrong angle.

I've had to evolve or medicate.

And by doing so a pattern has begun to emerge. One I'm grateful for. Parenting is a constant cycle of reacting – reflecting – unlearning.

Let me explain.

Say you react to something in the way you were shown as a child; your child does something wrong like hit their sibling and take their toy away. You react by snatching it back and shouting. After you've shouted and made the situation worse, it's time, if you're able to see it, to reflect on whether that was the best course of action and how it might have concluded with a more peaceful approach. Once reflected upon it's then possible to unlearn that reaction so you're equipped with a better strategy for next time.

It's taken me a long time to come to this realisation and I absolutely still get it wrong. And that's okay. I'm constantly looking for new ways to learn about my boys and how I can better understand their needs. I often sit and watch them play, with as little interference as possible, even if it gets heated. I literally sit, observe, and feel closer to them, sometimes gaining a greater understanding of their personalities. In the space of fifteen minutes they live through so many emotions. It must be exhausting for them. It's exhausting for me! It's a wonder *I* don't take a nap during the day myself.

Taking a hands-on approach to parenting has brought up so much stuff from my childhood which I'd simply underlined as, *that's just the way it goes.* When in fact, trauma can disguise itself in many forms. Addiction and anger being just two lovely little issues I've battled with for as long as I can remember. Picking at all these scabs from the past is not what I signed up for when I became a parent, but I wouldn't change it. It's made me a better person. More forgiving to myself and others. Even if I've decided to end certain relationships because of the knowledge I've acquired, it doesn't mean I haven't forgiven them. It just means I've developed a new set of ground rules for myself and my family which no longer includes negative or dysfunctional relationships.

Reacting – reflecting – unlearning.

It's not a bad mantra for life in general and you're free to steal it. It's possibly the only piece of advice or parenting tip I've got to offer. The rest is usually more like, try not to hit your kids in public and it's probably better not to drink booze before 11am.

GOING MAINSTREAM

I had a vision of the dad I was going to be. It involved being zen-like in my approach to behaviour management; no need for raised voices. I would intuitively decipher my child's emotions – bring about calming resolutions with empathy and patience. Gentle parenting. I was going to be the gentlest parent ever! Gentle but fair. Approachable. Open to negotiation. Bedtimes were going to be magical. I was going to tuck my little one into bed after story time, kiss his clammy forehead, switch on the night-light and leave him to fall asleep independently. He'd be secure in the knowledge mum and dad were downstairs drinking herbal tea and listening to *The Chimp Paradox* on Audible. Understanding ourselves was going to help us understand the needs of our children.

Ha! Nonsense.

That vision was obliterated very early on. Along with many other things like going gluten free, not using technology as a third parent, veganism, bribery, the list goes on. Even though so many things have changed, been removed, shifted around or sneakily brought back into play, there was one thing I didn't foresee changing. Our plan to home educate was a plan set in stone. Immoveable. It was never supposed to change. We had designed so much of our life around this idea that we never stopped to consider it wouldn't happen.

The plan was simple; after nursery, Arlo would attend a Forest School once or twice a week. We'd find some clubs: Performing arts, swimming, whatever Arlo wanted. Because being cool, child-led parents we were going to be democratic in our approach to education. He would have time at home with us to learn about the important things like cleaning the fridge, washing clothes, ironing clothes, making beds, cooking tea. The list was endless.

This boy was going to be ready to move out by the age of 10!

As it turned out, Arlo really wanted to go to school. *Really* wanted to go. We wouldn't be cool, child-led parents if we didn't listen to him, would we? We live around the corner from a primary school and each day Arlo watched the children walking in their uniform towards it and he wouldn't stop asking about it.

'Where are all those children going?'
'School, Son.'
'I want to go.'
'Really?'
'Yeah.'
'You have to go five days a week.'
'I don't mind.'
'You have to do as you're told.'

That got him thinking.

'You have to sit behind a desk most of the day and listen to the teacher.'
'Not all day though?'
'No, not all day.'
'You get to play with your friends sometimes?'
'You do.'
'I love playing with my friends.'

The home-schooling community offers a wide range of opportunities to meet up and socialise with other children. You get discounts for events and attractions within term time. Plus, several other perks and you aren't restricted by inflated holiday prices which is a massive bonus. But Arlo had a few negative experiences with some older children and, although they were isolated incidents, it left us feeling slightly put off by the idea of home-ed.

In the end we attended two open days at different primary schools, and he didn't want to leave either one. He loved the smart uniforms, classrooms packed with children. Young energetic teachers filled with hope wearing freshly ironed, stainless clothes. All smiling and happy. Maybe they were faking it? We couldn't tell. Either way, Arlo saw this world and wanted to be part of it. We couldn't ignore this. It was a curve ball we did not expect.

I'll admit it, I didn't want him to go. I'll also admit this; it was partly for selfish reasons. I was going to miss him. He's just so little. In Scandinavian schools the children don't start until the age of seven. I would prefer that. Arlo's just a baby, barely four-years old. He's super vulnerable; brimming with an infectious enthusiasm for life which can sometimes cause communication problems with other children. Sometimes with adults too. They don't know how to handle him. I was scared that he'd be bullied if I'm honest. I wanted to protect him for as long as possible.

But I'm also a realist.

I know I can't be there for him forever. But mainstream school kind of feels like the final nail in the coffin of our alternative lifestyle choices. What's next? Am I going to start eating white bread again? Shiny ham? Watching football again? Maybe I'll just get a mundane nine-to-five in a boring office where I can eat my white bread, shiny ham butties and talk about last night's game!

I know, I'm working through some issues.

Okay, there were some positives to consider. I have a few self-employment opportunities I could pursue with a little more enthusiasm. And there is this writing malarkey I dip in and out of. And I do have Ove, who is just a baby, and is kind of my responsibility while The Wife is at university. I'm batch cooking like a pro. The house is looking reasonably clean, and the ironing bag only weighs about half-a-tonne now which is a vast improvement. I found a shirt the other day I had completely forgot I still owned. I was like, no way, I look amazing in this shirt! The garden and mud kitchen look organised, and the car no longer resembles the bottom of a skip. Things are looking good. But do I actually care about those things? Not really. I'd much prefer to have Arlo at home with me. I'm selfish like that.

BONDING WITHOUT BOOBS

While preparing for the birth of Arlo, The Wife and I thought we had it covered. From hypnobirthing, homebirth, to half inflated birth pools, it was all under control. After the birth, The Wife was going to make cakes, drink sparkling wine and sleep for eight hours a night while our calm bundle of joy slept *right through*. Ah, to dream!

One *minor* issue we forgot to discuss, was . . . me. What was my job once he arrived? We planned the pregnancy, the birth, and The Wife was going to be his meal ticket, but we never discussed what it would be like for me. What type of dad was I going to be? What was my role?

It was so clear leading up to the birth. Feed the wife, scratch her back, and say nice things. Assist with difficult jobs like putting socks on and making cheese on toast, in that special way only I seem to know how. I also had a defined role during the birth. The knowledge gained during hypnobirth training gave me responsibility. I was able to whisper words and phrases of encouragement into The Wife's ear that reminded her how amazing she was doing and that everything was alright.

Watching The Wife transform into a warrior moving from bed, to floor, to on-top of the wardrobe and back again was something I'll never forget. Eventually she found her way into the birthing pool and I have no idea how much time passed but at some point Arlo's head was visible under the water. I kind of looked around the room at the midwife and asked with my eyes whether it was normal to have your head under water for this long, but she didn't appear bothered so I just went along with it. Moments later and a little purple, slimy baby popped out into the water like a torpedo.

Passing Arlo into The Wife's arms was a life changing experience and the relief, after all the appointments and pregnancy chat leading up to that moment, was huge. It went better than I'd expected but in the same breath, it was still super intense and scary.

Once the medical bits and bobs were sorted, The Wife relaxed skin-to-skin with Arlo and after a while it was my turn. Finally, I was able to experience the first snippets of physical entanglement with my son. Amazing. Beautiful. Later, close to sunrise, I was knackered and suddenly had an unexpected thought; *what do I do now?*

He was too small to play Poker and too young to drink wine. *What do I do now?* What a silly thought. I brushed it away and we all slept for a while. I woke three hours later feeling refreshed and excited about the day ahead. Becca emerged from her pit and got in on the skin-to-skin action too. The three of them shared some time together while my man duties began. Clean the room, empty the pool, and cook nice food. Crack open a bottle of sparkly and greet the few guests who came and went. It was a relaxed couple of days. Then things started to get a bit stressful. Arlo was struggling to latch onto The Wife's nipple and her breasts were becoming engorged. She was in pain. He was distressed. I felt completely useless.

Eventually, when we were contemplating buying formula, it happened. He fed and that boy has hardly been off the boob since! However, doubt reared its ugly head again.

How do I emulate a feeling that comes so naturally to her? How do I bond without boobs? I suddenly felt like an intruder and I can't sensibly explain why. I changed his nappies and tried to comfort him the best I could, but he only seemed happy with a boob in his mouth.

That's ma boy!

It's one of those overlooked issues I think. A bottle-fed baby gets passed around like a spliff at a party, everyone gets a go, before it's returned to the person who made it. And rightly so. Breastfed babies are like those spoilt kids who make you sit and wait on the floor while they have extra turns on their Sega Mega Drive because, "It's my game!" Spoilt! You know who you are.

In my head, not being able to feed him seemed to take a bonding opportunity away from me. Was I being selfish? Immature? Jealous maybe? The problem was I wasn't educated in the ways of breast-feeding. I'd never known anyone who breastfed or considered that it would affect our lives so significantly. And it did. The Wife was finishing her degree that year and when Arlo was six months old, he was with me for roughly four hours a day, three to four times per week. The Wife expressed, which wasn't fun for her, but it provided Arlo with just enough liquid nectar until she came home. So there I was, giving him a bottle of expressed milk like I'd wanted to and I realised, it wasn't comfort to him, it was just fuel. Once he was finished, he'd discard the bottle like it was a rotten banana skin. I couldn't use the bottle in the same way The Wife used the boobs. It wasn't the same. I had to find my own way.

This is where sling wearing really worked for me. And, being the master of distraction, I found myself doing a variety of things I never expected to connect with him. Funny faces and fart noises, no problem. But what calmed him the most, was singing. I was self-conscious at first, and rightly so, I'd never sang out loud as an adult unless intoxicated and reading the words off a screen, but I worked through it. I made up silly songs about poo, flowers, the weather, willies, you name it, I've got a lyric. I can sing *Five Little Ducks* in a variety of accents now. I even added a new verse with monkeys. As he crawled I could chase him from room to room, over and over and over again until my shredded knees could take no more. Mama might have milky boobs but she doesn't have kneecaps made of steel! Now he's a toddler weighing around 20st of pure chub, I get a free workout while throwing him in the air and dancing around the kitchen to *Rage Against the Machine* (a band he likes for reasons unexplained) while making tea.

We have certain games we play outside and around the house that are just for us. I know his expressions. I know when to calm it down and when he needs a snack. I've learnt this and more through trial and error. He forgives me quickly when I make a mistake the same way I forgive him when he smashes a book or wooden toy into my face when I least expect it for the millionth time.

He's my son and I'm his dad and one day when he's bigger I'm gonna tell him all about those feelings so that one day, if he ever becomes a dad himself, he'll know it's okay to be vulnerable. He can bond without boobs. I might leave out the toy smashing in the face bit though. Don't want to ruin all the surprises.

BEING DAD

For reasons which are unbeknown to him, he has never cried from happiness. Shedding a tear about something painful is hard enough so crying from happiness is very unlikely. There's been many opportunities but the urge, or need, or response, just doesn't arise inside him. But he wants it to. Isn't that a normal response to the emotional experience's parents encounter in their family lives? Watching his wife walk down the aisle towards him on a perfect day surrounded by close family and friends would have been such an opportunity. But nothing. Supporting his wife while she home birthed his children is another. More than supported. He took part in it. His sweat merged with hers. She hung from his shoulders. They breathed in nature's magic together. He experienced the great relief of holding both his warrior wife and healthy baby... but still... nothing.

No tears of joy, of relief, no tears of anything! It never happened. He's just not wired that way. Anymore. He's learnt to accept that about himself. He remembers tears of pain streaming down his young face as a small child - hurt and alone in his room trying to make deals with whatever supernatural force might be passing by. He can see his teenage years so clearly – screaming at the sky and smashing his fists against the walls, unable to understand the unfairness of life. Then his twenties arrived, and bank of tears had run dry. Instead of shouting, he danced with shiny chemicals inside him which had no time for frustration or sadness. But over time, as his relationships became more complicated and he shared his life with others, the bank of tears was replenished but the vault was locked and the key broken.

This meant developing strategies to prevent the tear bank from becoming overwhelmed. The vault was fitted with a combination lock; one that can be opened with a little forward thinking and just the right combination of factors to release the pressure. He achieves this by observing his feelings. Takes note. Recognises when the vault needs a release. Then, he acts. There're a few essential items required to help him open the vault just enough to ease the pressure but not let it run it dry again. This is a process designed through trial and error, over several years of experimentation.

Essential Factors:

- Two bottles of red wine. Minimum.
- Rolling tobacco and liquorice papers.
- Quiet, tidy, undisturbed space.
- Access to different genres of film (Independent films seem to work the best).

The Process:

His wife goes to bed, taking the two boys with her. He tidies up the carnage which has been littered throughout the house. He cleans the kitchen and fills the dishwasher while the red wine breathes. When his jobs are complete, he settles in front of the television, drinks, chooses a suitable film and drinks some more.

Happiness and sadness begin to merge as he watches a selection of films with the right emotional kick. He drinks his wine and has the occasional smoke. He pays very little attention to his phone and remains focused on the present; hoping to find the perfect combination.

It's not always successful.

At least twice a year, he'll find the *perfect* combination in this drunken state which unlocks the vault for a short time. Not a blubbery type of crying, nothing that would get out of control, just a comfortable flow of tears released as he watches whatever drama is unfolding on the television which has combined with the wine to complete the job. Afterwards, he'll watch the rest of the film, maybe watch another, finish his wine then go to bed with a warm satisfied feeling inside his belly. And for an undesignated period, while the vault is slowly filling up again, he'll be just fine. But always watching. Checking on himself. Ready for next time. Hoping that one day he won't need a process or a list of essential factors to unlock the bank of tears.

NIPPLES WITH PURPOSE

I've been staring up at the ceiling for over two hours while trying to get Ove to sleep. I know every single inch of it: The strange bit of crusty something that looks a bit like Jesus which the Sunday Sport Newspaper would have paid good money to photograph once, the dead spider in the corner, a lump of jam, I think. I've plotted a route through every bump, swirl, and crack from above the door-way, which I hope to escape through, and the window, which I'm considering jumping headfirst out of. But I can't escape. Ove, the boy who was supposed to sleep is furiously sucking on his diddy and using my nipple as a comforter. Vigorously!

Ha-ha. I asked for this. I actually asked for this by telling The Wife we needed a change. And what a change we've made. She's down-stairs sipping wine, dipping crisps into moist things, laughing her arse off watching YouTube videos while I'm being used and abused. Why couldn't I be one of those inconsiderate dads? I know loads of them, and their lives are amazing! I tell these lucky bastards about some of the ways we co-parent and how we work as a team, this is usually while having the occasional pint when I'm allowed to go out, and most of the time they just stare at me in utter disbelief. It's just not on their radars to lie in bed for over two hours while their kid twiddles, rubs and pinches their nipple until it no longer resembles a nipple. It's just a scab now. A strange scab that was useless but now has a purpose.

I don't want nipples with purpose!

It's a sacrifice I was willing to make because I didn't think Ove would care about my purposeless nipples. I'd never used them for anything myself. It never occurred to me that he would consider them an adequate substitute for The Wife's lovely boobs. But I was wrong. So terribly, terribly wrong.

But, we had to make a change. The Wife had Arlo clawing at her chest for three years and Ove was supposed to be different. Everyone said, "You never get the same kid twice."

Wrong!

She endured three years with Arlo sucking the last drips of moisture from her body then nearly two years of it happening all over again with the other one. And they don't just lie there suckling calmly. Oh no! These beasts want to twist around, do the crab, to drink upside down while walking up the wall. Still attached! Not once did either one of them just have a refreshing drink from each boob, thank The Wife, then go about their day redecorating the walls with yogurt and unidentified stickiness.

It's all or nothing with these boys.

I used to be the one downstairs drinking wine and living my best life now I'm stuck here staring at the flipping ceiling dying for a wee but scared to go to soon. He hasn't moved for twelve minutes now. His grip on my scabby nipple has gone limp; always a good sign. His breathing is loud and annoying. Way over the top. Arlo's at the other end of the double mattress completely knocked out snoring equally as loud. We never thought the day would come that he would be classed as the "good" sleeper.

We never believed we'd have a second child with recurring ear infections either. No one deserves that kind of torture. It appears we were wrong. But surviving one sleep thief has equipped us with a few valuable lessons. Don't think just because the little beast hasn't moved for a few minutes that he's sleeping. They like to do this fake breathing thing once they've accepted that the good shapely bit of your nipple has turned to mush, and there's nothing left to twiddle. Their breathing becomes rhythmic. The room calms. You start thinking about that wine. You allow the sensations in your body to return to normal because your bladder is set to burst.

It's a deception!

Why don't I just get up and leave? I'm glad you asked. If I just get up now and head to the door without checking if he's asleep first, and he's lying there all chubby faced and wide eyed, this would have been for nothing and I'll be stuck here for another hour, easy. Might as well kiss those crisps and dips goodbye!

So I won't be moving a muscle for at least another five minutes. I'm not even going to turn my head to see if he's looking at me. I'm going to stay right here, watery eyed and annoyed for another five minutes, at least, then I'll sneak and peek.

The Wife's laughing again, downstairs.

Nothing's that funny.

Go on.

Drink the wine.

Eat the crisps.

Make sure you don't choke!

God I need a wee.

That's it. Sod it. I'm making a move. I turn my head. I half expect to see Ove's blue eyes shining at me in the darkness but they're not. He's sleeping. No doubt. I know that look. Now for the tricky manoeuvre, navigating the spring in the mattress that is louder than a sonic boom and makes the most dramatic *boing* sound imaginable. Especially when I'm making my escape.

Gentle roll to my left, straight off the bed, landing on all fours like a cat in one fluid, well-rehearsed, movement.

No *boing* today.

Next, the squeaky floorboards between the door and my freedom. The trick here is to stay as close to the wall as possible. The carpet is less worn, and the boards are sturdier. Now in a press up position, I stretch across the room with my right arm and leg and, in one swift, acrobatic movement, I move across the space and push myself into a standing position with my back flat against the wall.

Then wait.

Five seconds.

Don't breathe.

I look down at my beautiful boys and pray I don't see their faces again until at least 7am. Now, the freedom shuffle. I edge towards the door. The floorboards groan a little, but the soothing classical music covers my tracks. I reach out and push the door and it opens effortlessly, and silently, because I drown the hinges with WD40 every flipping night.

Oh, I can taste that wine.

I continue with the freedom shuffle towards the adult world that's calling to me. *Come, drink, smoke, and fiddle with The Wife's ear-lobe. Come. COME!* One final look over my shoulder, oh shit, oh shit, the monitor, the flipping monitor, I've not switched it on. You idiot! You rookie! Sod it, they'll be fine... but they won't.

I know what must be done.

It must be switched on.

I must go back.

I need to be able to hear the slightest sniff of them waking up. The slightest deviation in their breathing. An out of place groan or sniffle, and I'll be up in a shot with a dummy and warm milk so it doesn't turn into an absolute screaming nightmare.

I need that monitor switched on.

I'm going back in.

I make my way back into the darkness, reverse freedom shuffle, but for some cruel joke of the Gods, every floorboard seems to be creaking louder than a theatrical barn door in a storm.

CREAK. Shuffle. CREAK. Shuffle. CREEEEAAAAK.

Why have you forsaken me, cruel Gods? I've done loads of bad things. You should be rewarding me for my sins.

Arlo just kicked Ove in the leg. Ove kicks him back. They're jostling for position. The great top and tail battle has begun. All I can do is watch and hope it doesn't escalate.

As quickly as it began it ends. Both boys flip on their sides and face the wall away from me. I hold my breath, sweat drips off my nose. My armpits are burning and stinking. This is my moment. I lean down, stretching with a finesse I didn't know my hamstrings would allow, flick the switch on then turn and dive straight out of the room onto the landing, closing the door gently with a touch from an outstretched toe as I fly gracefully through the air face first onto the floor.

I don't move.

The dust settles.

A minute passes.

Nothing. I get up off the floor. My bones are aching. My nipples feel like they've been involved in a nipple twisting marathon. But I made it. Two and a half hours. I could literally have watched Lord of the Rings or flown to Spain in that time, but none of that matters now because I made it! The boys could wake up at any moment, so now, I will commence with drinking two and a half hours' worth of red wine in less than fifteen minutes! Goodnight.

THE TODDLER AND
THE TELLY

We sold our television. And it felt amazing! The thought of not having one was a little alternative – even for home birthing, baby wearing, co-sleeping parents like us. But the notion kept recurring, could we live without a telly? We watched it sporadically – the odd boxset here and there. But the truth was, we were tired of arranging our living space to incorporate this electrical device. And once Arlo started marching into the living room demanding to watch *Paw Patrol* for the hundredth time in a day, we started to think seriously about it. Could we do it? Will people think we're weird? Do we care?

At three-years old, Arlo lived most of his life with chronic ear pain. You know how that feels? Ear and tooth pain have a very debilitating effect and, unfortunately, his condition was misdiagnosed – meaning he suffered greatly. When you've been up six times during the night, every night, to comfort him while he screams in agony, let me just say, there's not a lot of energy left for building blocks or Lego. We survived the first eighteen months before Arlo knew what the strange black object attached to the wall was. I think The Wife was reading some book on raising *less* annoying tech-addicted kids or something at the time. Anyhow, we played a lot of music and spent our time interacting with Arlo through play and the telly just wasn't used during the day.

He'd look up at it.

I'd watch his mind ticking away.

Not quite a mirror, not a toy.

'What is dat, Daddy?'
'Never mind, Son. Go back to being cute.'

Slowly but surely, as the relentless ear infections dominated our lives, it became a tool – one utilised in emergencies in the middle of the night or when needing a moments peace so I could, I don't know, wash the dishes, tidy the living room, sit quietly facing the wall! Maybe The Wife could plan some lessons at the dining room table without those sticky little hands clambering all over her and the laptop!

So, we gave in. We smashed the emergency glass, retrieved the remote control, and put on the biggest regret of my life – *Paw Patrol*. That song still plays within the deep recesses of my mind… I can hear it now, *Paw Patrol, Paw Patrol, be there on the double…* stop it, stop it! Let me live! Pull yourself together, force it back into the abyss with the opening soundtrack from *Friends* goddamit!

One hour became two. Once a day became three times. In the end, there didn't seem to be a moment when the telly wasn't on. The house had never been cleaner! His health would improve but then the weather got worse. We had to stay in and wait for a delivery. I needed to fix something; there was always a reason to switch it on and he became a full-blown addict. Creating a whole new problem. Arlo would come thundering down the stairs, all blurry eyed and chubby. A bottle of milk in one hand, something sticky in the other.

'Paw Patrol.'

I'd try and reason with him.

'Why don't we play for a bit, Pudding Chops.'

He'd look at me like I was the biggest dick head to ever walk the Earth.

'PAW PATROL, NOW.'

I love that boy but there was a thought creeping into my mind; could we give him back somehow? Offer him to science maybe? Ove was still a few months away from birth, maybe we could put all our energies into the new one and put this snotty nosed telly addict down to a failed experiment? The Wife disagreed. The Boy stayed.

This meant a change was inevitable. I had to find a way to parent without relying on the television whenever I was tired or needed to complete my dad chores. I was sick of watching him stare at the screen - literally expressionless and open mouthed.

'Fancy going to the park, Arlo?'
'Nah. Don't interrupt me until lunch.'

Three-years old and already done with play! Once, the mere mention of the park, even in passing conversation would result in him flying out the door with his wellies on, but he didn't want to go anywhere or do anything. It was my duty to get tough. Tough but fair.

The next morning when he came downstairs, there was a blanket over the telly.

'It's broken, Son.'

The easiest lie I've ever told.

Were you expecting some type of holistic approach? Maybe a bribe to comfort him? Nope. I unplugged the television; told him it was broke then sold it a few days later. We could live without it too. He was devastated. He screamed. Threw himself to the floor. Bit his fingers in protest. He wanted to get my tools out of the garage and fix it.

'Some things can't be fixed, Son.'

Absolutely true and a good life lesson to learn I reckon.

Without the telly to rely on, I began taking note of his behaviour. What triggers reminded him the television wasn't there. How tiredness pushed his thoughts towards technology. I saw how easily I'd been saying yes and turning it on. I'd played my part in this, but I was motivated to make it right.

It took three days to wean him off. He got angry when he remembered it was no longer there. He became upset. Threw stuff, and generally become very unpleasant to be around. Then, it was like a button had been pushed and he was back to himself. We read together more, listened to music, played instruments. I found games and toys that interested him again, and I lowered my expectations concerning my ability to parent and complete my dad chores at the same time.

Then Ove arrived. Desperation eventually followed as he developed into a sleep thief and I compromised by reintroducing some technology back into our lives. Just a small portable DVD player. A harmless, easy to manage, portable DVD player.

Now we have two addicts demanding to watch *Paw Patrol!*

(We lasted two years without the telly before buying another one. It wasn't because of the annoying kids in the end. It was after we'd shared a delightful stomach bug with the boys, and in-between running to the toilet to let-loose or puking not so quietly into a bowl in the corner, we spent most of the days in one stinky bedroom, dehydrated, bored, and huddled around that tiny portable DVD player watching an array of kids' films. Once the life returned to my body and I dared to wee standing up again, I said sod it, we're getting a telly. And yet again, I hate it.)

CO-SLEEPING WITH TWO

The thought of having a second child in the bed with us produces a twitchy, shuddery, *I can't bare it, please not again* kind of reaction within me. Outwardly I just smile when The Wife says things like "It's going to be amazing, snuggling next to our two babies all night." One part of me understands that warm feeling she's evoking because when Arlo's not clawing at her boobs, screaming for milk, waking every fifty minutes, thrashing around, or slapping me in the face with his big fleshy arm in the middle of the night, while he dictates who has any space in the bed – in the rare few moments when he's not doing that, yeah, it's quite pleasurable.

My main concern is space. We already gave up sleeping on a bed and opted for sheep skin rugs on the floor. Sounds a bit Viking-like but believe me, it's good for posture and we love it… now. It was a tough sell though. The Wife was not happy with the idea. There'd been a few issues with beds and mattresses in the past. Possibly my fault. We'd spent hundreds on different styles of mattresses, and I could not get comfortable on any of them. The last one we tried was some super-duper springy thing with a thin memory foam layer which seemed to finally hit the spot but on the second night I realised if I continued sleeping on that mattress, I was going to be crippled for life.

'At last. We finally got the right one,' The Wife said as we read side by side in bed.

'Hmm mm.'

Out of the corner of my eye I saw The Wife place her book down on the lap. I turned a page from Life of Pi, nervously, praying to the Almighty for a change in subject. Please change the subject! Don't ask me about the mattress.

'What?' She asked.

'I hate it I hate it I hate it I hate it I hate it!'

'Oh for fu… you said you liked it.'

'I lied because we'd had sex and I could've been lying on a pile of broken bricks and been comfy.'

'I give up. You truly are the Princess and the Pea.'

'I can't help it.'

'So, what are we supposed to do know?'

'I've been doing a bit of research and… this might seem a little extreme.'

'Oh my god, what is it?'

'Well, the bed's not really big enough for us when Arlo's in it as well, and with another one on the way how about this… no bed?'

Words are insufficient for the way she looked at me at that moment.

I was prepared to fight for my right for comfort. Some key advantages to sleeping on the floor were as follows:

The baby couldn't fall out of bed.

We would have the equivalent of a King Size bed without the cost.

No annoying wooden plinths to smack your shins on when drunk.

Cats couldn't shit under it.

I would stop moaning. Hopefully. Probably.

'There's one tiny issue all the bloggers seem unanimous on though?' I continued.

'Go on.'

'The first three nights are apparently a bit…'

'What?'

'Horrendous. But on the fourth night the discomfort vanishes as your body adapts.'

'So let's get this straight. You want to remove the expensive bed and sleep on the floor?'

'Not on the floor exactly. Sheep-skin rugs.'

That was the tipping point. The Wife's eyes darted from side to side as electrical signals in her brain fired from one synapsis to another. Her body went into shock. Unable to move. The expression on her face appeared to be one of mild disgust mixed with confusion. Have you ever smelt one of your farts and wondered how something so utterly vile can come from your own body? You look around the room hoping to blame it on a dying dog as your brain struggles to understand the situation. You don't have a dog. You're alone. The fart is yours.

That expression stayed on The Wife's face even after I'd kissed her goodnight on the cheek and turned the light off.

Becca ended up getting a very expensive bed for a fourteen-year-old and we found our way onto the sheep-skin rugs on the floor. The first three days were horrendous, as we had been told. For three nights I pretended it wasn't that bad. The Wife was not so accommodating. A suitcase had appeared in the room on the fourth night before we went to sleep, and half the contents of my wardrobe were stuffed inside. The message was very clear. This was the Princess and the Pea's final hurrah.

Hallelujah! The bloggers were right. The fourth night was amazing. Even Arlo seemed to have a slightly better night that usual. In the morning the suitcase was gone and The Wife liked me again.

'I told you it would be okay,' I said. Possibly a bit smug.

'Let's not get too excited just yet Miss Pea? It's not as if we haven't been here before.'

Fair point.

When the sheep-skin rugs were spread out on the floor with a blanket and huge sheet over them, the space was much larger than a double bed. Had we finally found the perfect co-sleeping solution?

No.

As it turns out the more space you give a kid, the more it'll take. We have met other co-sleeping parents and the general consensus is, the children ask for their own space naturally around the age of four. Arlo's two and a bit and there's another one on the way. I really don't think I can wait that long. He's showing zero desire to fly the nest and sleep in his own bed. I bought one of them tent thingies from Ikea to go over the top of his, so it looks like a cool den. But nothing. Within an hour he's out of it and pounding along the landing towards our room where he then spends the night wriggling, kicking and moaning his way through the night.

Can we really cope with another one in the bed?

Like it or not I've had to accept this situation because the alternative means one of us getting out of bed dozens of times a night to deal with him. Or the old school approach of controlled crying which, no matter how many times he slaps and kicks me in the night, doesn't appeal. He clearly needs our support. When he reaches out for me in the night and whispers "Dadda," or leans over in the morning and kisses me on the cheek, it fills me with love that I somehow turn into strength which gets me through another day.

But two of them… shudder!

CONVERSATION WITH A TEENAGER

It's Friday evening and I walk into the kitchen ready to open a bottle of red. The Wife's choosing a film to watch, and the boys are in bed before 7pm which makes this a great night. Becca's making smashed avocado on toast and wearing her comfy clothes which have more stains on than a washing powder advert. Her hair's tied up and she's watching *Friends* on her phone; all the tell-tale signs she's staying in.

'You staying in tonight?' I ask anyway.
'Yeah,' she says. 'Just chilling.'
'That's not like you.'
'I know. I'm tired.'
'We're just about to watch a film if you fancy it? We can watch something shit just for you.'
'Arr, thanks. I might do later.'
'It's nice to have you here on a Friday. We never usually see you.'
'I know.'

I swiftly open the wine and grab two glasses.

'Did you get the washing out of the machine?' she asks.

If I had a pound coin for every time I've asked her that very question, I'd be swimming like Scrooge McDuck now. Diving headfirst into a pile of coins.

'Seriously? I'm literally about to sit down.'

She doesn't bother to look at me. Chandler Bing is about to do something funny.

'But I need some clothes for tomorrow.'
'You've got loads of clothes.'
'I need a red top.'
'A red top? That's so silly.'
'Can you sort it please?'
'Can't you do it?'
'I'm making some food.'

She pauses *Friends*, turns, and gives me a look of pure helplessness. A but *I'm so tired* look. Her bottom lip doesn't exactly tremble because she's too good, but it's there. Just a whiff. In her defence, she's just started a new job. She's knackered. I'm not. What the hell.

'Right, I'll do it now.'
'Thanks.'

Friends back on. End of conversation. I take the wine into the lounge and place it on the small table which has only one purpose in existence; to look after my wine and make sure I don't have to stretch very far to get it.

'I've got to put the washing out,' I tell The Wife.
'Put it out tomorrow.'
'Becca wants to put some in.'
'Get her to do it.'
'I tried.'

'What?'

'Never mind, I'm doing it. Back in ten.'

In record time I arrive back in the lounge just as Becca blows past me like a hurricane of smells and hair, wearing a bright red top and chatting on a video call.

'I'm staying out tonight. See you later.'

Door opens and slams shut. We don't see or hear from her for three days.

A LOCKDOWN STORY

Depression almost wrapped its dark tentacles around my mind recently. It's happened before. Many times in-fact, but I'm taking steps to minimise the chances of it occurring again, because I really like being happy. I've curated a wellness toolkit which keeps me on the right side of positivity. Mostly. Sometimes I forget where I've put the toolkit, resulting in several days wandering around the house looking under discarded toys, the sofa, inside the wine bottles, in every place but within me where it lives. When I find it and look inside the feeling is on a parr with being a kid and opening a discarded birthday card, one you had considered to have a low to zero chance of financial gain, only to discover a tenner inside.

Once I begin examining the contents of the toolkit I remember why I have one, and the negative path I've been on becomes clearer.

I've been stuck in a cycle. I can step out of it. I can remember.

The tools appear like old friends who smile warmly.

'Hey, Fresh Air, how you doing?'
'You've been smoking again,' Fresh Air says a little judgementally.
'Yes, but I was thinking about you the whole time.'

I take a few deep intakes of breath and remember.

Next comes out an old, confused, haggard looking friend who needs a little extra care. I rest the tool down on a small rug, made by tribeswomen from some unheard-of part of the world, with crystals I have no idea how to use, and squeeze Meditation's shoulder reassuringly.

'Have we met?' Meditation hesitates. 'I recognise your face.'
'Yes, old friend. We are well met.'

We smile at each other. The sun bursts through the window covering the room with bright light at precisely the right moment.

'Do I have to go back in the box?' Meditation asks.
'No,' I say with promise. 'Not for a while,' in truth.

I sit peacefully and remember.

The tools don't only help me sustain a happy life in the present, they've aided me with retracing depressive threads from my past which have a profound effect on my thought processes and well-being. Having a supportive partner and being a dad have been the catalysts for great change within me. But it's come at a cost of forcing these threads out into the open and confronting what's at the end. If you ever reach his point and you've not considered vital tools like talk therapy, positive lifestyle change, or reflection, you could end repeating the cycle over and over. It gets harder to return to that sweet place called denial.

Depression is sneaky!

It's an opportunist. And once I'd made the subconscious decision to dropkick some tools back into the toolkit, because I tricked myself into thinking I could take a well-earned break, depression was waiting in the shadows, hungry and ready to pounce. But this has not been a normal life experience. I think we can say, without question, Lockdown March 2020 was nothing like we had ever experienced before. I won't share my opinions on the politics of lockdown, but I will say this - it felt like a holiday at first. Sparkling wine might as well have been flowing from the tap to my glass, which put me in a delightful mood until about 6pm when I had to reignite that buzz with a vodka tonic. It became a bit of a pattern of behaviour. Nowhere to go, unlimited food and drink and amazing sunshine every day. Sounds like the dictionary term for an all-in-clusive holiday to me.

The sun has always been a trigger for consuming more alcohol in the UK. It's our blood right. But as lockdown dragged on, I started to notice a dependency emerging. One that began to sour my mood and affect the way I was parenting my boys. It's not like I drank wine all day, every day, and *completely* ignored my kids. Lockdown measures allowed for outdoor exercise once a day which we took advantage of by strolling around our local parks and small trails and paths filled with litter and dog shit. That was depressing enough. We had to think outside the box. Find new ways to enjoy the outdoors without the use of the play areas which were closed, by den making, bird spotting (God forgive me) and a hundred variations of hide and seek.

At home we had water fights, paddling pools, and lots of bubbles. We had ice creams and ice lollies. Every meal or snack felt like it was part of an all you can eat buffet. I was using white crusty bread loaded with butter instead of cutlery to shovel several forms of salad, meat and dippy things into my constantly open mouth. Cheese and crackers. Cakes. Fruit smoothies. Chocolate in a hundred different forms seemed to appear magically in my hand. I was getting cases of wine delivered every two weeks rather than once a year! We discovered a love for vodka orange because it made The Wife and I feel light and giggly. Oh, and cider because when it's hot you just got to have a cider. It's the law.

All this consumption. All these earthy pleasures designed to give me a quick fix. A short relief from the global fear being shoved down our throats. The fear. The lockdowns. The boredom. The consumption! All accumulated into a moment of clarity once I remembered where my toolkit was.

The Wife and I came to an understanding - the drink needed to be put back into its place. Two nights a week maximum. We returned to intermittent fasting, which we both value, and the only treats allowed in the house, a part from crisps of course, were home baked. No more easy-to-reach sugary snacks. No more tipsy, easy to manipulate parenting either! The kids were mortified. They couldn't understand why the holiday was over. How life had suddenly been put on hold and our all-inclusive holiday had begun was confusing enough for them. One day they had school, friends, routines and the next it ended. Replaced with this strange new life based within the confines of the home with their watery eyed parents who now had a sudden tendency to say yes to everything and wore the same stained shorts and t-shirts every day while listening to *Fleetwood Mac* very loudly.

The motivation for change came once we realised the boys were morphing into rule phobic wild beasts addicted to ice lollies and the third *Aladdin* movie no one's seen, ever! The realisation coincided with lockdown restrictions being eased which gave us more freedom to travel further afield. It helped with the monotony of trying to make the visit to the same park, for the seventh time in a week, more interesting than it was. Gaining this slight freedom raised all of our positivity levels and for me personally, I was able to look rationally at my own mental health and see how I'd locked my wellness toolkit away with my running shoes and the ability to locate a snack not wrapped in plastic.

It felt good to be me again.

SURVIVING THE SUMMER

I've always loved the summer. More than any other season. Crusty skin peeling off my Irish heritage white nose and forehead. Dealing with the constant threat of running out of ice cubes. *All* the windows open *all* the time. Duvets in the cupboard. Heatwaves that last weeks. The smell of freshly cut grass. Water fights. Long days. All that stuff. The Wife sees things differently. She's the kind of positive person who appreciates each season.

'All the seasons have a special role to play. Spring is about renewal and…'
'Let me stop you there, Babe, I don't care.'

I'm not interested. I'll take a little bit of autumn and the best bits of spring, but those long dark days of winter just drag. Maybe I'd enjoy it more if we hibernated; months spent getting fat on barbecued food, washed down with Swedish Mixed Berry Ciders, made from crystal-clear freshwater springs which are in-fact melting glaciers! Each day from the beginning of March right through to the end of August, gorging on high fat greasy foods and sugary everything's. Six pack stomachs are for losers and the fatter you are the more desirable you become to skinny members of the opposite sex who will need to rely on licking your salty sweat to survive the winter months locked in your bedroom with a portable loo and a couple of Amazon Fire Tablets.

Summer's amazing. The mornings were the best when I was a kid and they got even better in my twenties. I'd open my eyes and immediately know it was going to be a good day. I'd stretch. Scratch a bit. Pretend to meditate for five minutes, then open the curtains fully and embrace the day. There was always an air of possibility about what lay ahead. Not that I actually achieved much but the feeling was always there. I'd watch the human activity outside, already in full swing as if it was lunch time. Derek the flat cap guy washing his car, again! Kids chalking nice things on the pavements, like flowers and love hearts. Cats motionless on a fence waiting to torment and dismember a pigeon. The sky, cloudless and blue, stretched as far as the eye could see.

Work was even fun back then too because it was with some mates and we'd all go to the pub at lunch to have a few pints. Returning to work forty-five minutes later - red faced and smiley. Eager to smash out the next couple of hours of production so we could escape as soon as humanly possible. After work we'd pile in the cars and head straight to the pub where there was the very real possibility of getting extremely messy until silly O'clock in the morning.

After a few stolen hours of sleep my eyes would open suddenly. The alarm would sound a split second later. Sweat, dehydration, and humidity glued me to the bed sheets. Fifteen minutes to get up and ready. Nah. Snooze button! This gave my mind enough time to replay the previous days events in a reasonably coherent order. Alarm again. One more snooze. I can be ready in five minutes no problem. Then the best bit. Lying there focused on the glass of water on the bedside cabinet. Always out of reach physically and mentally. My brain screaming for moisture. Cracked lips and a tongue wrapped in concrete. When body and consciousness got it together and I could muster the cognitive power to reach over and take it, to quench that thirst, then it was time to get up and repeat!

Now when I feel that early morning humidity and open my eyes, I see two young children leaning over me like menacing shadows of expectation.

'Can we get up now?' Arlo asks.
'Give me a second, Son. I've just woken up.'

Three seconds.

'Can we get up now?'
'Okay boys. Let's be quiet, don't want to wake your fake sleeping mum, do we?'

She doesn't move an inch. She's a pro.

Summer now consists of locating shade and water during the day and surviving with two (already well documented) sleep thieves, through the night. And night doesn't come at the usual strict time of 7pm does it? Oh no. The kids don't believe that it's bedtime.

'But It's still light?' Arlo says.
'It does that in the summer.'
'I want to play outside.'
'Mummy and Daddy want to drink wine.'
'Me and Ove want to watch a film.'
'You just said you wanted to play outside.'

Long pause. He considers his options.

'Here's the deal. Let us watch one more film.'
'And what? Where's the bit I want?'

Long pause.

'I'll give you 10p.'
'Bed. Now.'

Longer days ruin our watertight bedtime routine which is a massive problem for me because I don't want to see any kids face between the hours of 7pm and 7am. Evening time is adult time. For doing grown up stuff like tidying up the kitchenware that finds its way into the garden, littered amongst every pillow, cushion, and blanket you own. And toys. Lots and lots of spikey toys that love sticking in your bare, I'm so grounded right now, feet. After those jobs you unload the dishwasher for the fifth time then guess what? You flipping load it again, wipe the sides, find ten more used glasses scattered around the lounge and wash them in the sink. You take the washing off the line, (three lots dried in a day, get in!) then you open the wine, get the snacks ready and chill in the garden with your partner for a few blessed minutes before the children wake up screaming because they're too hot, over tired, bla, bla, bla.

In the end it's not worth staying up so we go to bed and bring them into our room. It's too much hassle getting up thirty times in one night to attend to their woes. So, we end up with four humans fighting for a cold patch in one sleeping space. I peel Arlo's sweaty leg off my own every couple of minutes, tearing it off like soggy Velcro, pleading with him to please stop touching me. Watching The Wife's blank expression as the industrial sized fans blow warm air into her face from several directions while Ove tries to claw the final droplets of milk from her crusty nipples. She already went through this with Arlo. Watching her endure it again breaks my heart.

'I love you, babe.' I whisper.
'This is your fault.'
'How's it my fault?'
'There's something wrong with them. This isn't normal,' she hisses back.
'Whoa, chill out. I know there's something wrong with them but why automatically assume it's from my side of the gene pool?'
'Becca never did any of this. No one else's kids do this! All night. Every night.'
'Gentle parenting.'

'What?'

'I blame it on gentle parenting, we should have-'

'We should have what? Beat them? Used fear or bribery?'

'I'm just saying-'

'Well don't.'

A long pause.

'I meant controlled crying. We should have done that controlled crying thing.'

The way she sucks in air through her nostrils tells me that was the wrong thing to say.

'Go away, now.'

I tiptoe out of the room and never mention it again.

WHEN THE WORLD MADE SENSE

Remember when Shrek wished for a single day without any parenting responsibility? A day he could return to his free-spirited youth, running half naked around his swamp with a Porn Star Martini at 11am on a Wednesday morning after a busy night slapping around the simple folk. A single day when taking a poo in peace (a PIP) without kids banging at the door was his basic right.

He just wanted a day *when the world made sense*. His words

Shrek looked around and recognised only predictability and routine. The reality of parenthood, sleep deprivation, and pairing socks overshadowed the positive aspects of being in the present with his family. His discontentment grew until he eventually snapped!

I totally get it.

Imagine having one day to live your old life again. It's not like Shrek asked for much. One measly day. Parenting beat the imagination out of him. Twenty-four hours released from the shackles of responsibility does sound appealing. Most parents I speak too would probably just sleep – wake up the next day refreshed and say it was worth it. I once thought this was crazy talk. Like when people won't have a beer because it's a "school night!" But now I get it. Oh how I get it now!

How do you make your wishes? Do you grit your teeth, squeeze your eyes shut and plead with the almighty to intervene? Do you make big wishes? Or are you the quiet type? Muttering small almost insignificant wishes under your breath regularly because you don't really expect anyone to help? However you do it, I warn you, be careful what you ask for. One day the planets might align and grant it. And that could be the beginning of a long and painful period in your life you just aren't mentally equipped to handle.

I know this because it happened to me.

One dark winter's night many moons ago, a sentence was uttered. An empathetic gesture which was taken literally.

'I wish I could help more with the bedtime routine,' I said quietly whilst gently shaking my head.

This was *so* obviously just a show of emotional support. But there was trickery afoot on this cold dark night as my words caught a draught and echoed loudly off the walls.

I wish I could help more with the bedtime routine!

The lights flickered.

The Wife raised her head. Her pale face obscured by the greasy matted hair streaked across it. Her eyes… those tired red eyes. Those desperate eyes. I'll never forget them. That mixture of suffering, pity, and gratefulness. I'd made this wish before but this time the twitching and her right hand crushing the arm of the chair told me it had been granted.

'Yeeeessssss.'
'Erm, what was that, Dear?'

I headed swiftly towards the kitchen.

'Need to put some olive oil in my ears, I'm going deaf.'

I wriggled my finger inside my ear for effect.

The kitchen door was only a metre away. The light behind it felt safe. Welcoming. Like everything from the past thirty seconds would be erased if I could just get to it. Get behind it into the warm glow of safety. But I didn't move quickly enough. I blinked and she was in front of me. Her hot primal breath overpowering my personal space.

'You can help with the bedtime routine.'

She stepped even closer.

'Mooore.'

Sweat ran cold down my spine. My balls ached. I felt sick.

Ove, now resembling a wild creature rather than a baby, looked at me with his fierce blue eyes and soaking wet everything. I reached a loving hand towards *it,* hoping to offer *it* some comfort as *it* squirmed in The Wife's arms but only rage and tears sprung from every atom of *it's* being. Before I could back away The Wife had already unloaded *it* onto me.

Silence filled the air. That deafening silence that replaces chaos. Ear ringing silence!

I looked down at the wild creature. We shared a psychic connection. A knowing. We both knew life was never going to be the same again. I started to panic as my new reality began to merge with the old. I wanted to tell her that I'd opened wine. That I was about to watch a film and chill out. How I'm such a better daytime parent.

It didn't matter.

There was a flash of movement ahead as the hallway door at the other end of the lounge crashed open and a dark shape moved through it out of the room. I raced with Ove towards the hallway, stopping at the threshold and peering into the darkness.

'Babe,' I whispered.

I patted the wall searching for the light switch but hesitated when I found it.

'Where are-'

Ove kicked out, straightening his body flatter than a plank! I accidentally pushed the light switch before dropping to my knees, catching him in the process. I rolled onto my back as the dull LED light fitting illuminated the stairway.

I couldn't see her at first, but I could hear strange crunching and slurping noises. As my eyes adjusted, I finally saw The Wife under the stairs devouring snacks from Arlo's nursery bag.

'Easy now, eeeasy.'

She leapt onto the banister, turned, hissed, then pounced up the stairs, taking several at a time. The bedroom door slammed shut. There was a heavy thud, some incoherent muttering then a noise so uncanny I have no simile to describe it – I can only surmise that it was the sound of snoring.

I looked down at my son. I loved this boy. I had no problem getting him to sleep during the day. How hard can it be to do it at night?

Six months later…

I have no concept of time… of self… I often consider crying… I only sweat under one armpit, never both, and he uses my scabby nipple as a comforter. These could be the final coherent words I manage to send from my brain to my… erm, what were we talking about? Something about Shrek making a wish? Or was it me? Was I in Shrek? Who are you?

It has begun!

THE SNIP

'I don't wanna.'

'Condoms it is then.'

'There must be another option?'

'Nothing.'

'How about that temperature thing?'

'Oh yeah, I'll check my temperature before we have sex then hope for the best. Good one.'

'But the snip seems so drastic. So final.'

'It's a minor incision. You'll be in and out in half an hour.'

'But...'

'What?'

'Nuffin.'

'What is it?'

'It's stupid.'

'I'm prepared for that.'

'It's two things.'

'Give me the lesser of the two first.'

'Okay. What if it comes out weird? What if it's disgusting?'

'I have some news for you, Husband, it's already disgusting.'

'You know what I mean?'

'I know exactly what you mean and unless you get fitted with some chocolate sauce producing balls it's always going to be disgusting.'

'What if it's all thin and weird?'

'Rather than thick and gloopy? I'd say that was an improvement.'
'I knew you'd be insensitive. That's why I didn't want to say anything.'
'I'm being as sensitive as I possibly can considering I gave birth to your second child less than a week ago.'
'It's not coming across as sensitivity.'
'I'm not going to indulge this ridiculousness.'
'It's not ridiculous to me. Imagine having an operation-'
'Minor procedure.'
'An operation which suddenly changes the colour of your blood?'
'Why would I want to change the colour of my blood?'
'You don't, that's the point.'
'You've lost me.'
'You don't get it.'
'You've got that right.'
'I'm trying to talk about a genuine fear and you're laughing at me.'
'Trust me, I'm not laughing.'

Silence.

'I'm sorry if you think I'm laughing. I'm not. I just don't think you're being very rational.'
'I don't think I am either. I'm having a lot of crazy thoughts.'
'What was the second thing?'
'Ay?'
'You said there was two things on your mind.'
'Oh. Promise you won't laugh?'
'I'll try my best.'
'I can't shake this idea that it'll stop me from... erm...'
'What?'
'From you know?'
'I have no idea.'
'That it's going to be like cutting off the source of my horny powers. Once I've been snipped, I won't feel the urge for sexy time anymore. I'll end up being like those other blokes who would rather play five-a-side footy with their mates. Or worse, I'll get one of them chairs and sit for hours playing shooting games online with a headset on.

There I said it. If I get the snip that's going to happen. Is that what you want?'

'I'll take my chances. I'm booking the appointment.'

And that was that.

Note to dads:

It was alright in the end. Relatively painless. There was a strange smell and a few tugging sensations. The doctor was very gentle. Afterwards I felt like I'd done a thousand sit-ups and tight underwear is the way to go. A week or so I conducted a small experiment of my own and, as it turns out, apart from a tiny bit of blood, all was still thick and gloopy and I'm still as horny as a teenager.

A LOCKDOWN STORY

I didn't know this pre-kids, but I was built for play. I'm that guy rocking a headscarf and colourful beads while the boys shuffle around in Mama's high heels. I take hide and seek very seriously, remaining hidden, breath held, till the very death or at least until bursting for a wee. I allow mess. Lots of mess. It's going to happen anyway, so I get on board and enjoy it. There's something liberating about dragging the folded towels and sheets from the shelves, adding them to a huge pile of duvets and pillows in the middle of the bedroom, then spending half a day constantly chucking the boys through the air onto it. They don't get bored and neither do I.

When lockdown was first introduced, we felt, as a family, well equipped to handle it. Our house is designed for play: Black board painted walls, dens everywhere! Art corners and a back garden stuffed with tuff trays, water play equipment and a mud kitchen. It felt like an extended weekend. Later nights. More telly than usual. Time to blow the dust off that *Learn Spanish in A Week* CD. Wine with tea? Wine with lunch more like. Add some glorious weather into the mix and that extended weekend evolved into an early summer holiday but with two differences: You couldn't go anywhere further than your local green space. You couldn't socialise.

It didn't take long before the cracks began to show. Parenting 24/7 was a tough slog. We'd fallen into the trap of overusing the word yes. It was *sooo* easy at first. The kids were loving it. But the holiday spirit ended once we started to reintroduce the word "no" again. The atmosphere quickly soured. Patience and tolerance were shelved. Play was a chore. We seemed to run out of ideas. So, as most parents will understand, we turned to the telly more and more. The good old third parent. The bringer of so much pleasure with a side order of addiction!

The third parent gave us a little peace. But it broke the boys. They malfunctioned, unable to maintain eyesight on anything but the telly. They suffered from a lack of coordination – ice lollies in the eye, juice straight onto their sticky bellies. Food scattered about in all directions. When they did bother to speak it was bossy and Neolithic.

'Dad, we hungry.'
'You've only just finished your third breakfast, Son. Look down, most of it's on your t-shirt.'

Eyes fixed on the third parent.

'We hungry now. Dad, get food now.'

It wasn't even 10am!

'I'll make you both lunch in an hour. Butties, crisps, and some chopped up apple. A mini picnic.'
'We want crisps and chopped up apple now. Dad, get or we make you sorry.'

And they did make us sorry. A lot. We had to get tough which meant turning off the telly and becoming active loving parents again. And with our boys, that means play. Lots of play. If they are not sufficiently entertained in some form or another, they begin ripping wallpaper off. Seriously trying to hurt each other. Drawing on paper is not enough, you need to build a den (which takes an hour) from the hundred Amazon boxes piled at the front door, so they can paint it using all the paints, all the crayons, all the yogurts before destroying it after five minutes. Then they stand there like, *now what?*

It was exhausting.

The Wife and I would tag each other in like beaten wrestlers. I'd take the 6am till 12pm slot and she'd have the little beasts until teatime. I'd arrive at the baby gate, bruised, sweating and dazed. I'd hang onto the gate then raise my hand in the air and wait for that slap of the hand – the tag – that sweet release from the relentless pummelling of my mind, body and patience by the little beasts. Then it would come. Tag!

The Wife, freshly dressed and watered, with a can-do look in her eye would slap herself around the face several times, stamp her feet then bunny hop over the gate into the pit of insanity. She'd grip my ankles and push me headfirst over the gate to relative safety. Never taking her eyes from the pile of cushions in the centre of the room, knowing a naked beast could attack with a large wooden spoon at any moment.

'What're you doing now? Writing? Painting the bathroom? Learning Spanish? Upskilling?'

The Wife would ask.

Me? I was already getting my supplies together.

'I'm off to the front garden with a bottle of Prosecco and some cheese.
'But it's barely midday.'
'I know. See ya!'

I'd leap from the kitchen window onto the boiling hot metal vehicle below, using my flabby body and a packet of Edam cheese slices to protect my champagne flute and cheap Prosecco from the impact. Anything to avoid parenting for a few hours.

24/7 parenting, with nowhere new to go, no one to see, created a tangible strain inside our home. We all felt it. As lockdown was eased, we travelled beyond our local area, exploring woods with streams to paddle in and hills to climb. This occupied us for most of the day and was the turning point that broke the monotony of lockdown. We found a way to balance yes and no again but it was tough going there for a while.

Some keys lessons were learnt: Drinking sparkling wine before lunch is not the best motivator long-term. You can't rely on the telly to parent your kids (I know, who knew?) and Amazon boxes do actually come in handy.

FLASH NON-FICTION

5am: I know he's awake. He's huffing, puffing, and rolling around in the covers like a baby crocodile ripping a gazelle to pieces. He pulls the duvet off me completely, exposing my cold battered body. I try to stay as fake asleep as possible and pull the cover back onto my side while making "I'm still asleep" noises.

It goes quiet. No movement. You never know, he might go back to sleep. Ha!

5:05am: He's literally breathing right down my ear. I can taste his breath inside my skull.

5:09am: It's gone quiet again. I take a chance and open one crusty eye. He's staring right at me. Shit!

'Dad.'

This pointless game is over.

'Good morning, Son.'
'Can we go downstairs and watch that film?'
'I used to class 5am as night-time you know?'

'The one when the mum and dad die when the tiger kills them and the baby cries in the treehouse.'
'I don't think it's a tiger.'
'And then he lives with the monkeys.'
'Gorillas.'
'What's it called again?'
'Tarzan.'
'That's it. Can we watch it?'
'No. Go back to sleep.'

He leans over my face and shares with me a continuous stream of thoughts, bargaining strategies, beliefs, and reasons why he should be allowed to watch Tarzan.

5:11am: His little brother enters the bedroom.

5:13am: Downstairs watching Tarzan.

DIRTY TALK

It's a rare, peaceful night. The boys were sound asleep, completely wiped out before I'd even finished reading the second book. They haven't woken up yet and it's nearly 10pm! That's a record. God it feels good to sit here under faded lights with a glass of red, an endless supply of crisps and The Wife.

I turn slightly to The Wife and smile. She smiles back.

'I don't remember the last time we watched a full film all the way through without having to check on the boys a hundred times,' I point out.
'I know. It usually takes about four hours to watch one film.'
'This is nice.'
'It is.'

We watch the rest of the film, drink our wine, munch our crisps.

Fifteen minutes later the film finishes, and the boys still haven't woken up. The baby monitor crackles away in the corner of the room, oddly quiet for the first time in its existence. This is uncharted territory. The second bottle of wine's been drunk. We can't open a third. Can we?

'Is that all the wine?'

The Wife shakes her empty glass for effect.

'It's the last of the bottle, not the last of the wine.'

I watch The Wife complete a risk assessment in her head. She's calculating whether it's possible to throw caution to the wind and get super pissed. Can we stay up later than 11pm? Are we pushing it? Will the kids wake up and start screaming the moment we open the next bottle? Will one of them suddenly develop croup? One will definitely wake up during the night, so how drunk is irresponsible drunk? We deserve one late night though don't we? It's Saturday tomorrow, they can watch telly all day, and eat rubbish while we lie in bed, all dehydrated and sweaty.

We could call it a lazy day.

Unlikely.

Once she's completed the calculation, her expression informs me it's time for bed.

'We better not,' she says.

I take her glass and place it with my own on the side table. I smooch up a little closer, gently push her back into the warmth of the sofa and begin to kiss her neck.

'One day, do you know what I'm going to do?' I whisper into her ear.
'What?'
'I'm going to find someone to babysit those boys for a full night.'
'Stop teasing.'
'I mean it. Then, I'm going to book us into a fancy hotel.'
'Yeah.'
'An old one with a four-poster bed. A massive one.'

'Then what?'

She strokes my back and pulls me tighter as I continue to gently kiss her neck and earlobe.

'We'll pay for an early check in and a chilled bottle of sparkling to be waiting in the room.'
'And some chocolates?'
'Yeah, hundreds of chocolates.'
'And we'll drink the wine and eat the chocolates,' The Wife says all breathy. 'Then…?'
'Then I'll pull back the heavy duvet. I'll guide you over to the bed and undress you slowly.'
'Then?'
'Then I'll pull the duvet over you, close the curtains and put a do not disturb sign on the door. Then slide in behind you and snuggle you so hard… then sleep!'
'For how long?'

There're tears in her eyes.

'All night, baby.'
'All night?' she mouths.
'And most of the day depending what time we check in.'
'I want it so bad.'
'I know.'

The baby monitor shrieks to life with a child's cry and reality returns. The Wife's up in a flash and heading towards the door like the amazing mum she is. She turns before exiting the room.

'I'll hold you to that, Husband.'
'It's a promise.'

She's still waiting…

BEING DAD

Sometimes, usually when he's tired and splattered in paint and sticky things, he thinks about what his life was like before parenthood. A life without structure. No real purpose. Except the pursuit of drink, drugs, and short-term physical connection which all the other aspects of his life revolved around: Job, no job, new job, drink, drugs, sex, holidays, nights out, days out, weekends out! Little bit of selfcare for short, intense, periods of time: Meditation, gym, healthy eating, healthy thinking, healthy living!

The reason his mind wanders into the past, he thinks, is because there's a small part of him that's waiting for it to return. That some-how, someone, is going to point out he's not a responsible adult yet and it's all been a mistake. It's like a section of his brain believes the part of himself, the bit he didn't need to share with anyone, will return and the purposeless life with no structure can continue where it left off.

But the real him, the mind behind the mind, doesn't really want that old life back. Sometimes he's just tired of being a parent. Tired of being responsible. When he looks back he knows that although life might have been lacking some depth, it was also easy, and every now and again he could do with a bit of easy. Couldn't everyone? Don't we all need a bit of easy sometimes?

When he was a kid, being a parent seemed simple enough. Most of the adults smoked anywhere they wanted. Drank anytime they wanted. Had parties. Went on holiday without their kids. He spent a lot of time at his Grandparents with his brothers where the food on offer was usually unhealthy and delicious. Lots of meats and fatty foods, and white bread with everything! Entertainment was limited. They had a couple of video tapes to choose from which they watched over and over again but that was alright because they didn't know any better.

No one ever took the time to explain things to him. He had to keep questions inside. Family secrets trickled out over time and confused him because he had to piece bits together himself. This often left him feeling more confused, but he just had to accept it.

It's not like that for his boys. All things must rotate around his children because they don't keep *things* inside. They let it *all* out from dawn to dusk every day. All plans, actions, most of the learning and conversation with his wife is based around their boys. They require a lot of attention. They don't seem able to just, *be*. External stimuli, whether that be food or entertainment, is always at the forefront of their minds. When he was a kid, he was happy to play at the bottom of the stairs with his action figures for as long as he was allowed. For him, that was his favourite thing to do and the less adult interference the better.

He knows he shouldn't look back and compare the parenting styles from the past to his own. It was a different world in the 80's and 90's. In-fact, comparing himself to anyone else is probably not helpful or necessary. Once he might have used language like, "I've made sacrifices for my boys." But now he thinks about "choices." He and his wife have gone without a steady income. They've gone without many things. The idea of rushing around each morning, sorting breakfast, teeth, clothes, books, bags and all that stuff before scrambling out of the door then reversing it all in the evening doesn't sit well with their world view. And sleep deprivation has showed them that it's impossible anyway. It's been difficult living on a tight budget, and on occasion, they've wondered whether they could have done it differently.

On the days when he's feeling sorry for himself because he's had very little sleep, no time with his wife, zero adult fun and the boys are being argumentative or simply annoying – he takes comfort in the phrase, "This too shall pass," which reminds him to find pleasure in the little things. To break the train of thought which is pushing him towards the past and do something fun now. Chase the boys around the house. Build a den. Shout, "I'm gonna bake a cake, who's with me?" And then be a rebel and eat some of it before teatime! He knows this time is precious, he just needed reminding every now and again.

The Sperm Collector

'I think I'm pregnant.'
'Hmm.'

I roll my eyes and continue searching Netflix for something to watch. I know what's coming next.

'Can you go to Morrisons and get me a test?'

I knew it.

'No.'
'Please?'

This scene has been played out many times before. For a woman who has already felt a child grow inside her, it's amazing how many times she gets wind confused with pregnancy.

'I'm going food shopping tomorrow. I'll get one then.'
'Don't you want to know whether I'm pregnant now?'
'No.'
'Babe!'
'Leave me alone. I've been looking for something to watch for about an hour. I'm going to see if I can break my record and get to two hours without finding anything. I'm very excited about it.'

I'm not sure how many pregnancy tests I've purchased over the last few months but definitely enough to play Jenga with. I'm tired of buying them. I repeat the same scenario each time I'm stood in the supermarket aisle talking to myself.

Me: 'Just buy two?'
Mind: 'But what if she's pregnant?'
Me: 'Then I'll be stuck with an extra one we don't need.'
Mind: 'Exactly. They're not cheap.'
Me: 'I could always bring it back to the shop?'
Mind: 'Haha. You can't be arsed doing that.'
Me: 'True. You know me so well.'

I don't have a problem going to the shop for my lovely wife, the shop is where I buy wine. It's the fact she, maybe this is pure coincidence, although I have my doubts, always asks me when I'm chilling out. Plus, I have my money on wind because of all the farting she pretends I can't hear, or smell.

There's one more reason I believe it's a waste of time.

'Babe.'

I sit up straight and put on my most serious face.

'I've never said this out loud, but I don't think I can have kids.'

She pulls a funny face and stares at me for ages.

Mind: 'She thinks you've got a STD.'
Me: 'That's impossible.'
Mind: 'Is it?'
Me: 'We've been together for years so yes.'
Mind: 'She thinks you're a freak.'
Me: 'No she doesn't.'
Mind: 'Maybe you are?'
Me: 'Will you piss off!'

She places a supportive hand on mine.

'What makes you think that?'

I detail, as tactfully as a husband can, a delightful little tale about many sexual partners and a total disregard for contraception. The fact none had come forward baring a small child with my undeniable charm and good looks. How I've never received a friend request from an unknown child or mother asking me to supply school trousers and an iPhone. This evidence plus years of drink and drug use, can only mean one thing.

'I'm barren.'
'Men can't be...'

The Wife squeezes my hand and speaks softly.

'You're going to have to do it in a cup.'
'Ay?'
'I'm making you an appointment at the family clinic. You're getting tested.'

"Do it in a cup." She makes it sound so easy. Just do it in a cup, no candles, soft music or even a bath. Who does she think I am? A teenager. I thought I'd left cups, socks, pillow slips and all that behind me.

'Do I have to?'

'Yes. It's the only way to be sure.'

'Can you come with me?'

'No way.'

'Why not?'

'I have to go for a smear test on my own – you get to do this.'

'What if I can't cum.'

'I'm sure you'll power through. Like an athlete crossing the finishing line.'

As it turned out, I didn't have to stand in a poorly lit room at the doctors romancing myself while looking through a Country Life Magazine. I was able to take the little pot home with me and complete the deed while The Wife stood outside the bedroom shouting, "Can I come in yet? I need to dry my hair." She gave me a whole ten minutes. No pressure. Luckily for me I had eight minutes to spare. I was already avoiding my shameful reflection in the mirror by the time she barged in.

Not really. I waved the cup of goo in her face.

'It's still warm, touch it.'

'Piss off you dirty boy.'

A week or so later I received my results. My sperm was fine. I had a few lazy ones apparently, not willing to take on the hazardous journey, and a healthy percentage ready to invade The Wife's inhospitable environment at any moment. There was nothing to be concerned about. No heavy drinking. Don't romance myself, if possible, too often. Don't smoke crack and with a bit of nature's will we were good to go. This was encouraging news. I felt positive. For The Wife, the news created more of a physical response. Basically, she couldn't keep her bloody hands off me!

If you'd have asked me at the time, how much sex I could handle, I'd probably have said I'm partial to a bit of morning sex for breakfast. A light lunch to recover then a sensual massage with oral sex for tea. And naughty drunk sex once or twice a week as well would be cool.

I was such a fool. Thirty-odd but with the brain of a teenager! Because you know what they say about quantity over quality don't you?

At first, it was amazing.

'Right, come on,' she'd whisper.

I'd be over in a shot. Kissing, cuddling, fondling our way to the eventual orgasm. It was bliss. Lovemaking at its best. For about a month, my life was so sweet. The Wife and I were mature students at the time. She took her studies very seriously. I have a more relaxed approach. Like drinking beer before midday. Smoking spliffs with the cool kids at uni. And some days, literally doing nothing. If I was feeling adventurous I'd clean the bathroom just for fun or find other ways to procrastinate, like rearrange the furniture. Anything that kept me away from completing my assignments.

The Wife took full advantage of my willingness to avoid my studies though. Sex in the kitchen, the garage – when I leased expected it. Morning, noon and night. I was living the dream.

Then one day, it all changed.

'Right, come on,' she ordered.

I slammed my laptop shut, leaped over the desk, rubbed some warmth into my hands - flipped a fresh mint into my grinning mouth and danced provocatively over to the bed like Patrick flipping Swayze. Smooth. Sexy. I lent down and took in the sight of my beautiful wife. I placed a loving hand on her cheek and kissed her tenderly on the lips.

'No time for any of that, just get on with it.'

'Erm, seriously?'
'I've got work to do.'

Wow! What did she think I was, a piece of meat? How rude. I must admit, as I began taking my trousers off, I felt a little cheap but I love The Wife so I did what I was told.

'Okay,' I said. 'Just this once.'

I can't lie. I struggled to enjoy it. She made it worse by constantly checking her watch and tutting during the act of lovemaking. But I'm a trooper. A professional. With a lot of concentration, plenty of toe curling, panting and butt clenching techniques – I was able to produce the sperm. This became the norm. From then on, even if I was tired, or if I wanted to talk about her day, or my feelings god-damit! It didn't matter. She might as well have had a whip, cracking it on the floor around my feet.

'Perform for me.'

CRACK CRACK CRACK

'Now!'

My favourite past time became a chore. I've never been the type to cry after sex, but it was getting close. My penis looked like it'd been used for Chinese burn practise. But she didn't care. I couldn't remember the last time we'd snuggled. She didn't seem bothered. Who was this beast? This woman on a mission was not the woman I'd fallen in love with. She was a machine. A sperm collecting machine. And if I didn't give it willingly, I think she would have surgically removed some while I slept.

'I'm a bit tired.' I said one night.
'Haha. Funny.'
'Seriously, I'm knackered.'
'Lie down.'

And that was it. That was the limit to my fight. After she'd had her way with me and told me to clean myself up, I realised something. Women are cruel when they want a baby!

CONVERSATIONS
WITH THE WIFE

'So?' I ask.

Long pause. Ridiculously long pause.

'Is there anything you want to say?'

She's looking directly into my eyes, sort of. She's gone kind of vacant. Like there's something behind me more interesting and the only way to see it is to imagine a hole in my head.

'Are you okay, Babe?'

Her left eye twitches.

'You don't have to say it. Your silence is enough.'

I wave her off like I'm not bothered.

But I am!

'You...'

Here it comes.

'Yes?'
'You…'

Come on. Say it!

'I'm what?'

Her throat ripples with the force of her dry swallowing.

'You were…'

She grasps the doorframe for support. I bet her head's spinning.

Just say it.

'You…'
'Say it!'
'Fine, you were right, I said it! You were right. The sofa looks better there.'
'And the table?'
'Yes. That too.'

I stride into the centre of the room like Russel Crowe in *Gladiator*, hands raised to the Gods. My imaginary crowd roars in celebration. Single stemmed flowers, and gold coins are thrown at my feet.

'Are you not entertained?'

I drop to my knees and clasp both hands together, shaking them to the sky.

'Mark this glorious day.'
'Calm yourself down.'

The Wife crashes through my victory parade and sits down on the sofa.

Nothing can ruin this occasion. I rise. I am… reborn.

'From this day forth, our relationship will never be the same.'
'If you say so.'
'Finally, we're equals.'
'Sure.'
'No need to thank me.'
'I didn't.'

Her eyes complete a full 360.

'Now go make me a brew,' The Wife commands.

You have no power here!

'I don't make the brews around here anymore. The tide has turned.
My brewing days are over.'
'Really?'

I leave my adoring fans and take a seat next to The Wife on the sofa
which is now resting in its optimum position in the corner of the
room. By the gods this is a glorious day.

'You're right again. Your brewing days are over.'
'Thank you for acknowledging that.'
'Change is in the air.'
'Isn't it.'
'There's been a shift. Especially since Ove was born.'
'Ay?'
'Yep. And now you've had the snip, my child baring days are over.
I can put my feet up. Job done. Is sex even necessary anymore? I
mean, what's the point?'

I'm already in the kitchen.

'How many biscuits do you want with your cup of tea, Dear?'

A FORCE OF NATURE

'Do we really need a doula?'

'I'm working through a lot of fear. I didn't think I was going to do this again.'

'But a doula? We're doing full circle and going from the alternative to mainstream again.'

'Having a doula's not mainstream.'

'Didn't Prince Whatever's wife have one?'

'I don't know. But that wouldn't make it mainstream. That just means she's taking control. Birthing the way she wants.'

'Whatever. What does a doula actually do?'

'Offers support. Helps to organise things on the night. She'll be able to prompt me in ways which we have already discussed. She'll-'

'Why can't I do that. I did it with Arlo.'

'I know, and you still will. It'll just be another birthing companion. She'll be there to support you too.'

'In what way?'

'We'll make plans before the birth. Discuss ways she can support you while you support me.'

'Like what?'

'I don't know. Off the top of my head, she can make us all cheese on toast while we do skin-to-skin with the baby.'

'Oh. Cool. I was thinking something like that but thought that'd be a bit cheeky.'

'Think of a doula as if it's a close family member. Someone you can trust to look after me but also someone you wouldn't mind asking to put the kettle on too.'
'Right. Sounds good. You got someone in mind I suppose?'
'Yeah. She's only £700 but-'
'£700. Forget it.'

The Wife is skilled at giving me the illusion of choice. She should work in politics. But in fairness, getting a doula was right for us. Where a midwife can offer medical, a doula is more about emotional support. Someone able to connect with birth more than I can. I'm the rubbing shoulders, do you want a glass of water, is the baby here yet kind of birthing partner.

It's 11:52pm. I open my eyes. The Wife is two inches from my face parallel to me in bed. Bit close for comfort, especially since we had garlic bread for tea.

'What's up?'
'I think the baby's coming.'

I can't help but roll my eyeballs dramatically. Don't judge me – she's said this quite a few times recently and it always ends up being a trump.

'I've been awake for an hour. The baby's coming.'

I switch the lamp on and slip into my imaginary doctor's coat. I place a hand on her belly. I touch her head. Her knee.

'What are you doing?'
'Checking you're alright.'
'I haven't fallen off a bike.'

Something is different tonight. Her complexion. The way she's looking at me. During the pregnancy she's developed a selection of facial expressions that inform me what she's thinking. Raised eyebrows and stretched cheekbones - she's forgotten something downstairs. *You don't need to get it immediately but don't bother getting into bed until you do.* Scrunched-up nose and tight lips – she's hungry and wants cheese on toast. *You don't need to get it immediately but don't bother getting into bed until you do.*

She looks calm but excited now; aware and determined. Her eyes are sparkly with anticipation. I'm shitting myself. You can do as much prep as you want but when this moment arrives, it's difficult to describe. It's a mixture fear and excitement. Like taking ecstasy for the first time or waiting to go on a rollercoaster while watching other people on it screaming in horror.

The key here by the way is preparation. Oh my days have we pre-pared the shit out of this. With Arlo we got stuck into some alter-native thinking: Hypno-birthing, home birthing etc. I don't mind sharing this with you, The Wife will probably never read this bit, but I'm totally bored talking about birth, boobs and encapsulating placentas.

I rush downstairs and grab my list off the fridge. I need to calm down. No point getting stressed out. First job is to call our One2One midwife. Then fill the birthing pool with warm water. Not above 37.5 ℃. That is circled several times on the list. Midwife first.

'Hi. It's Adam Glennon. I'm trying to contact our midwife-'
'Emma's not on call tonight. I'm Sarah. I have all your details.'
'What are the chances of that? Never mind. That's fine. We've prepared for this.'
'How's Claire doing?'
'She began experiencing surges about an hour ago.'
'Okay. It will probably be a few hours yet before you need me to come. Keep me updated on her progress and I'll get organised.'
'No worries, speak to you later.'

I run back upstairs, taking two at a time. Calm down, calm down.

'Got a bit of news, Babe. Emma's not on call tonight.'

The Wife's on all fours on the floor.

'That's fine. Did you call Elle?'

The doula!

'Next job on my list.'
'Okay. Is the midwife en route?'
'She said keep her updated.'
'Call her back. The baby's coming.'
'She said it's unlikely to be within the next few hours.'
'Caaaaalllll heeeer back, nooooow,' The Wife hisses, whispers but
also shouts.

I nod and slowly back out of the door.

'Hi, Sarah. The Wife's ask me to call you back.'
'Oh. Is it her first baby?'

I thought you had all our info?

'No. She's already prowling around the bedroom floor like a lioness.'
'I'll set off now. Should be there within the hour.'
'Great. I'll leave the front door ajar. Just let yourself in.'

Doula next. Then the pool!

'Elle. It's happening.'
'I'll be there in twenty minutes.'
'Amazing.'

Into the lounge to fully inflate the birthing pool which has been
sitting in the corner for the last week. For the last baby I nearly
killed myself blowing it up under pressure. Not this time.

I grab the small electric pump from the draw and attach it to the side of the pool.

One minute later: Done. Oh yes!

The rest of my list consists of sheets and towel preparation, lights, music, food, and drinks. But filling the pool is next. I catch myself starting to rush again then slow down and walk into the kitchen. Everything I need to fill the pool is under the sink. Already tried and tested. So why oh why does the hosepipe adaptor suddenly not fit on the tap? I checked it the other day and checked it again! Water is pissing out from all angles and it won't fit in the right position. I turn the water off and try again.

I'm sweating now. The pool is a fundamental part of the plan. I look down at the adaptor in my hand and give it another go. Useless. I stare at it. I will it to fit but as it turns out, you can't weld rubber and metal together with a stern look and hope.

'Babe,' The Wife shouts from upstairs.
'I will never forgive you,' I tell the traitorous adaptor.

I drop it in the sink and run up the stairs. I smell like a mixture of cabbage and raw meat.

'Little boy.'

Arlo's stood outside the bedroom rubbing his eyes and wearing the floppiest hairdo ever.

'What you doing?'

He points to the bedroom where The Wife is currently making some animalistic noises. I pick up Arlo and turn towards The Teenager's door just as she appears from her fortress of tech and incense.

'Perfect timing. Can you take him?'

'Come here, little boy,' The Teenager says. 'Shall we watch a film on my bed? I've got choccy.'

He pushes me away like an empty plate and they retreat into her room. We want them to join us as soon as the baby arrives so Arlo can see that the new person he's been talking too inside The Wife's belly isn't just the rumbling effects made by wind and packets upon packets of Rich Tea biscuits.

I open our bedroom door and step inside. The atmosphere's thick with energy. Something tangible's filling the room-like stepping off a plane into a new country and getting hit by the heat. The Wife's leaning against the wall.

'Are you okay, Babe? What do you need?'

'Water.'

I grab the pint glass off the cabinet and pass it to her. She's very hot. I open a window. It's only been about fifteen minutes since we were lying in bed but she looks like she's been in labour for hours.

'I'll get some fresh water and bring it up. Listen, Babe, the pool isn't gonna happen. The adaptor won't fit-'

'It doesn't matter. There wouldn't be time to fill it anyway. The baby's coming.'

That feels like a twenty-tonne rock's been lifted off my shoulders. I turn and Elle's padding slowly up the stairs with the birthing bag and bottled water. The Wife was right. Having a birthing companion is the right choice for us because watching her walk towards me now with the things I need is giving me a warm tickly feeling in my belly. I think it's called support.

'Elle. Your timing is, well, perfect.'

She smiles - takes some towels from the bag and places them in front of the armchair. The Wife and Elle whisper to one another then Elle helps The Wife remove her bra from under her t-shirt and holds her steady as she kicks off her pyjama bottoms. They hold hands for a moment then she unscrews the lid from the bottled water, holds it to The Wife's mouth as she swigs. Then Elle sits in the corner in a meditative position.

This is it. It's time for me to be completely present. I position myself to The Wife's side and begin slowly caressing her shoulders.

'You're doing amazing, Babe. Everything's great. Everything's okay.'
'Is everyone okay?'
'Everyone's fine, Babe. Arlo and The Teenager are watching a film and eating chocolate.'
'Okay.'

She begins to sway and moan. Unrepeatable swear words are used. She's completely uninhibited. She keeps checking in between her legs as if the baby's head must be hanging out. I'm no expert but I think she's being a bit keen there. She turns towards me. Her eyes are wild. I'm ragged from side to side by the scruff of the neck with such force, I grip the armchair to make sure I'm not thrown across the room. Her heightened primal strength is so present she could rip the doors off a car. Or even open the Christmas pickle jar which has been sealed in the fires of *Mordor*!

I relinquish any notion of control.

The Wife is so focussed. I think. Or lost. It's difficult know exactly what she's experiencing. I plant a knee and foot to the floor and grip the armchair. Her arms hang around my neck in a boxer's clinch. Our sweat and heat mix together.

I whisper into her ear, 'I love you. You're amazing.'

There's no sense of time. Nothing else matters. The Wife places a hand between her legs again and again I can't help but think it's too soon. I never really followed all that dilation stuff. But then she releases an ear-piercing scream and splosh… the baby hits the bedroom floor at our feet in a tangle of chord and plasma.

I can't believe it. I put my hands behind my head and look around the room for someone to confirm it's really happened. Elle nods and smiles. The Wife begins to bend for the baby, but I gently hold my arm out, reminding her to take what is known as a "birthing pause." A moment to take in the magnitude of what's been accomplished.

'Babe, you did it. You did it. That was amazing, that was…'

She strokes my face and I kiss her hands. The baby's little cry fills the air.

The Wife collects the baby, still attached to the cord, off the floor and sits in the armchair. Elle wraps a blanket around The Wife's shoulders. I'm just in awe at what I've just witnessed. There's a knock at the bedroom door. The midwife pops her head in and suggests coming back in half an hour to check everything's okay. The door opens a little wider and The Teenager and Arlo step into the room.

'Is it a girl?' The Teenager asks.

We had all predicted a girl. The Wife peeps underneath the towel.

'I can't tell.'
'Cake,' Arlo says.
'Come and meet the baby first.'

We all gather around this amazing woman and the smelly bundle of life in her arms.

'Actually, I'd love a piece of cake. And a brew,' The Wife says.

Before I can respond Elle is up and out of the door.

'I'll sort that.'
'Thank you,' I say.
'It smells,' Arlo points out.
'Is it a girl?' The Teenager asks again.

The Wife looks at me.

'Are you ready to know?' she asks.

I already know it's a boy because I'm either looking at some strange growth hanging between his slightly crossed legs or a huge weirdly coloured ball bag.

'Say hello to your little brother, Ove.'

FOR GRAPES SAKE

I'll be the first to admit my language has been a little blue over the years but having the boys is forcing me to rethink my word choices. It's not often I've let slip anything particularly vulgar but I'm finding it increasingly difficult to keep that adult language under wraps.

Day one: I entered the living room as Ove was using porridge to re-decorate a recently painted wall.

'For grapes sake, Ove, sit at the table.'
'No!'

Interfering in his life only motivates him further. He scooped out another handful of porridge from the bowl and turned his attention to the sofa. I considered reaching forward and stopping him but seriously, what's the fu… flipping point?

Day two: I'm juggling bags, coats, and children in my arms. It's raining. One of them is kicking off. I dropped the car keys on the floor outside the front door.

'Sausages!'

The kids looked at me weird. Even they thought it was pathetic. This charade's not going to last long. I'm not the kind of person who can get away with being nice all the time. But I don't want to swear around the boys. I need to retrain my brain by somehow removing years of council estate conditioning. A lifetime of bad language passed on from one generation to the next. It began at primary school where I was taught the basics in genitalia related swear words and accompanying hand signals. The words available evolved during secondary school and into adult life but becoming a dad changed many things and swearing less was one of them. But the urge to swear more often has returned with a vengeance now the boys consistently ignore my pleas for mercy.

Day three: I walked barefoot, what a rookie, out of the kitchen with a boring cup of tea in my hand and stood on the spikiest toy ever created! It stuck horribly into my *sole*. Shock waves shot through my leg, up my torso, causing my vocal cords to vibrate, releasing words into the world which ideally would have been *for grapes sake* but, unfortunately, were not.

I hobbled over to the armchair and found solace in the fact it wasn't red wine dribbling along my arm onto the carpet. I attempted to gauge what Arlo had heard while furiously rubbing my foot. He didn't seem bothered. Maybe I'd gotten away with that one?

A few hours later: The Wife was on the floor playing with the boys. The trainset had been expertly set up by Arlo but Ove, a destructive force, systematically destroyed all in his path. Before we could intervene, I heard my words repeated back to me.

'For grapes sake.'

(I hope we're all on board here, he didn't say grapes).

The Wife looked at me with one expertly arched eyebrow. I returned that arched eyebrow with an open mouthed, *oh my goodness, I'm shocked beyond words* kind of expression. *Where on earth would he pick up language like that? What has the world come to?* I shook my head and tried to find something else to look at. I eventually caved in and made eye contact with The Wife again and we engaged in a deep eyebrow to eyebrow psychic conversation.

"You knew I was a gobshite when we met," my left eyebrow and slight grin said.
"That's not a very mature defence," her raised eyebrows and twisted lips replied.

'Swearing has nothing to do with maturity,' I scoffed.

Her nostrils did a little dance, and I knew there was no point arguing about it. Our eyebrows agreed to not draw attention to it any further. Her gently nodding head informed me, *I'm still a good dad but I need to try better next time.* I agreed with a nod.

Next day: Arlo was doing his thing with the building blocks on a mat when Ove decides to obliterate it all.

'For grapes sake, Ove!' Arlo screamed.

I needed a word. I gently explained to Arlo how Daddy had used a grown-up word the other day and it wasn't bad, just not for children. I suggested using something different.

'Like what?'

I thought I'd shift it away from grapes or any other food related replacement.

'How about saying something like, flipping heck?'

We kind of shook on it. All day he muttered "Flipping heck" to himself while playing. Very cute. That evening: The Wife came home, and we enjoyed an incident free couple of hours. We were sitting at the table eating tea. All was well. Arlo leaned forward and simultaneously knocked over a glass of water and elbowed his fork, complete with tomato pasta shell, which went flying and splattered onto the floor.

'For grapes heck!' Arlo shouted.

I didn't need to look at The Wife to know her eyebrows were shouting at me again.

MELTDOWN TIMETABLE

06:30am
Arlo: 'Morning, Daddy.'
Me: 'Morning, Son.'
Arlo: 'Can I watch a film?'
Me: 'Not first thing, son.'
Meltdown Scale 6/10

06:52am
Arlo: 'Where's my breakfast?'
Me: 'I'm just sorting it now. Why don't you set the table?'
Arlo: 'I want chocolate.'
Me: 'You know we don't have chocolate first thing.'
Meltdown Scale 7/10

07:01am
Arlo: 'Where's Daddy gone?'
The Wife: 'He's feeding the cats.'
Arlo: 'Daddy said we could watch a film and have some chocolate.'
The Wife: 'I don't think so, Lovely Boy.'
Meltdown Scale 8/10

7:30am
Arlo: 'Will somebody play with me?'

Me: 'I'm just tidying the kitchen.'
The Wife: 'I'm going to do some yoga. Why don't we do it together?'
Arlo: 'You're both poo heads.'
Meltdown Scale 7/10

8:00am
Arlo: 'Can I have a snack?'
Me: 'You've just had breakfast.'
Arlo: 'I'm still hungry.'
Me: 'You're not just stuffing your face all day.'
Meltdown Scale 8/10 - Parent Meltdown 5/10

9:07am
Arlo: 'Can I have an ice-cream?'
The Wife: 'You've literally got a rice cake in your mouth.'
Arlo: 'But I want an ice-cream.'
The Wife: 'You're not having an ice-cream.'
Parent Meltdown level 6/10

9:28am
Me: 'Arlo, don't do that to your brother.'
Arlo: 'He likes it.'
Me: 'He's shouting no and trying to run away.'
Arlo: 'He likes it.'
Parent Meltdown Level 7/10

9:44am
Arlo: 'Can we watch the telly now?'
Me: 'We're going for a walk.'
Arlo: 'I want to watch the telly now!'
Me: 'How about this, I take the telly off the wall and smash it to pieces?'
Maximum Combined Meltdown 10/10

9:45am
Me: 'Yes to everything for the rest of the day.'
Kids: 'Yay!'

A LOCKDOWN STORY

'Babe! Babe,' I shout from the bathroom. 'You need to come see this.'

The Wife comes running towards me with a worried look in her eye.

'What's going on?'

I point down at the washing basket on the floor.

'Look.'

She follows the direction of my finger. I watch her facial expressions change as she moves from annoyed – confused – to enlightened. A look of pure happiness and surprise radiates from every cell in her being.

'It's empty,' she whispers.
'I know.' I place a supportive hand on her shoulder.
'Is this real?' she asks.

We both take a step closer to the empty basket and peek inside. The material is damp. A bit mouldy. It stinks in-fact but there it is, the bottom of the washing basket. I don't have to look at The Wife to know her eyes are filled with tears. I'm feeling emotional too.

'But that's not all,' I say.
'Nothing can top this day.'
'Follow me.'

I take her hand gently in my own and guide her upstairs past the spikey Lego pieces, over the sticky something and through the pile of soft toys and pillows, to our bedroom. The sun's radiation beams through the window and the clearest blue sky stretches as far as the eye can see. A large metallic clothes maiden is stretched out in front of the window. Sunlight reflects off it and dazzles our eyes. I don't even have to say the words.

'It's empty,' she whispers again.
'There's more.'

The Wife's eyebrows almost leap from her head as she opens her eyes wider than what should be possible for a human being. Our hands remain together, tighter, as I pull her from the room back towards the pile of soft toys and pillows. I spot Marshal from Paw Patrol and kick him in the head, The Wife uppercuts Peppa Pig in the face and we blast through the rest, sending them all flying through the air. We enter the kids bedroom and jump over the piss stained towel on the floor, over the crusts and half eaten soggy pear, over the pencil crayons, felt tips, dried out Play-Doh, over one of our paint smeared naked children, to the window which faces the garden.

'Loooook,' I whisper.

Again, she follows the direction of my pointed finger to the empty washing line hanging lifelessly between the house and the shed. The emotion is too much, and we embrace. We hold each other tight. Our hearts beat in unison. We know this feeling won't last but here and now in this moment, our lives have never been so in-tune. So complete.

We turn on our heels and float out of the room. Nothing can touch us. Our hands stay formed as one as we glide down the stairs together. Truly together. Oneness.

'What time is it?' The Wife asks.
'Nearly lunch time.'
'Too early for a glass of sparkling?'
'It's lockdown, Babe. It's never too early.'
'I'll grab a bottle from the garage and put it in the fridge.'
'I'll make lunch.'
'Perfect.'

I lean forward, we kiss passionately. It's almost impossible to separate our hands which have merged into one, but we manage it. I slide into the kitchen and open the fridge.

'What goes best with sparkling wine?'

I begin emptying the shelves of all things tasty and pile them on the worktop. I grab crisps. Fruit. Chocolate! This is going to be a fine feast.

'Daddy,' Arlo enters the room.
'Oh hi, Son. Has the film finished?'
'Not yet. Mummy's crying.'
'Tears of joy, Son.'
'I don't think so. She's on the floor.'
'Ay?'

I leave the feast, pick Arlo up and stride towards the playroom where the internal garage door is. The Wife's curled up on the floor in the doorway. She's not crying any longer, but her eyes are painfully red and her face is whiter than any face I've ever seen. I place Arlo on the sofa.

'Is mummy dying?'
'What? No, Son, just put your film back on.'

He switches the TV back on. I kneel slowly, placing a hand on her cold shaking shoulder.

'Babe. What is it?'

She mutters something.

'I can't hear you.'

She pulls her twitchy hand from her armpit and points into the garage. This time it's my turn to follow the direction of a pointed finger. The garage is gloomy, and jam packed. I don't see it.

'There…' she forces out the word only slightly louder than a breath.

My eyes adjust to the light and I see. Now I see. Oh my god it's enormous. The room begins to spin, and I grab for the doorframe just in time before losing my balance. I use it to pull myself into a standing position because if I let myself fall to the floor with The Wife there's a possibility I'll never get up again.

How did I not realise this would happen? How could I be so foolish? Such a rookie. A massive error in judgement. I need to see it properly. I need to face this head on. I scramble for the switch behind the door and flick it down. The light pierces my eyes for a moment, I'm blinded, but I push forward into the room and stop in front of the biggest pile of ironing I've ever seen in my life. It appears to be growing up the walls like a hive of fabric. There's a large Ikea shopping bag at the bottom that now looks tiny, ready to burst, straining against the sheer magnitude of the weight upon it.

What have I done… what… have I done?

MOVING HOUSE

Moving to a new house is supposed to be one of life's most stressful events. Top five some say. Personally, I think that's nonsense. This is stressful, having an overwhelming urge for hangover cheese on toast, mustering the motivation to leave the comfort of your stinky bed, dragging your feet to the kitchen, putting the grill on, making a brew, grating the cheese then opening the cupboard to find that some imbecile has eaten the last of the bread, but for some sick – twisted reason, has left the plastic bag there with nothing but crumbs inside.

I kid you not, these people exist. You might even live with one of them.

But I suppose stress it's subjective, like most things in life. Personally, I love packing. Organising the bejesus out of it. Getting rid of all the bits and pieces scattered or stored around the house which you've been clinging onto for reasons unknown, and finally have an excuse to sell or donate. It's like some unspoken right of every dad to remove anything he deems not worthy of keeping without discussing it with anyone.

'Have you seen the kid's Peppa Pig puzzle?'

'You mean the one that's been on the kitchen floor for a week?'

'It's not been a week.'

'Trust me, it was a week.'

'Where is it?'

'Gone.'

'Where?'

'You know where.'

'You've sold it?'

'This is a time for honesty, Babe. You're going to find a lot of things have moved on.'

'I knew it.'

'It's better this way. You have complete deniability with the kids.'

'I can't believe this. That wooden toolset?'

'Gone.'

'The plastic sand pit, that coconut instrument, my Spanish ceramic bowl… it's all becoming so clear now.'

'Yes, yes, and yes, Babe. You choose the new house, I decide what goes. It's my right.'

Kids don't get much of a say in this life changing event. How do you explain to little ones that you plan on uprooting them from the one place they call home to some strange empty house splattered with dodgy wallpaper and a kitchen with a subtle but noticeable smell of rotten cabbage? There are smells in all the rooms. An emptiness. A sense that other lives have been lived here and now it's your turn to fill that space. The kids don't understand why this is being thrust upon them. They were happy where they were. That box room which they'll eventually outgrow is theirs. They don't think about size. The scribbles on the walls are theirs. The den under the stairs. The tree out the back. It's the safest place they've ever known.

How do you explain to them that's it's a good idea to leave it all behind?

Gently is how. A tip-toe approach is probably best. Or even better, lie to them. When Arlo was three and Ove was a new-born, we got motivated and began the process of looking for a larger house. When you're a Social Housing tenant you can enter the crazy, and unpredictable world of home swapping. It's the only way to remain a social housing tenant and move. It's what's known as a mutual exchange. You tidy up your house for long enough to put some pictures on a website called Homeswapper. You have many, many conversations with people who have zero intension of moving but just enjoy playing with your emotions until you finally meet a few likeminded types who appear sane enough to be serious. They come to your house and you pretend your neighbour's not a complete nutter and you go to theirs and they pretend no one's ever been stabbed outside the shop.

You smile and explain how you just never, after three years, got around to painting over that horrendous orange colour in the bathroom and they smile and pretend the holes in the doors are from the kids playing with baseball bats, and we all just smile and bullshit our way to an unspoken agreement, that we know is all lies but we don't mind because we want a dining room, and they want a driveway.

Many obstacles can and do get in the way and people are free to change their minds at the last minute of course. Ha. Ha. Ha. Twice we were left with packed boxes and dismantled furniture after the moves fell through. We didn't achieve the "gently" bit, because we got organised far too early. We were naïve. We created a confusing atmosphere at home, especially once our possessions appeared back on the shelves. It was probably a mistake to take Arlo to view the potential home swaps because he never misses a trick and listens, even when it appears he isn't, to everything being said. *Won't this look good here? The kids will love this room* etc etc etc. It never occurred to us that it wouldn't happen because we were so determined to move to a new area. We built up the expectation then it crumbled around us, and we didn't know how to reverse all the promises we'd made.

It's difficult to say what Arlo understood, but the uncertainty played out in various behavioural patterns, like suddenly refusing to sleep in his bed because he no longer liked his room. Becoming fearful that ghosts were everywhere, preventing him from enjoying some independent play which he'd started to develop. He had taken a step backwards because there was suddenly an element of uncertainty in his life which hadn't been there before.

And then it happened. From out of nowhere we were contacted from someone who knew everything about our house, road, neighbourhood, and they wanted it! And they had a large town house which they couldn't manage. It felt too good to be true but we were guarded at first.

'I've literally just put new wardrobes in every bedroom. I thought we were staying?'
'Yeah, but… a town house?'
'I know, it sounds amazing but I can't be bothered with it all again.'
'Just look at the pictures.'
'I don't want to.'
'It's a town house, Babe.'
'I hear you, but…'
'Taaaawwwon house!'
'I know…'
'Town house.'
'I get…'
'Ta ta ta ta ta tawn hase.'
'Babe?'
'Ta ta ta ta town house!'
'Right, show me the flipping pictures.'
'Oooo, it has a garage!'

We signed on the dotted line and the process began all over again, but this time boxes were packed and stacked out of sight. We tried to keep the house looking as normal as possible until two days before the physical move, when the contracts had been signed and there was no backing out. Then we took Arlo round to see the amazing new house with three floors!

On moving day, I made sure there was lots of cake, nice drinks, Grandparents to play with and a new DVD for him to watch. This held his attention sufficiently while everything happened around him. Ove was a new-born and enjoyed draining every last drop of milk from The Wife so it was difficult for her to multi-task between parenting and organising as I unloaded box after box into each room.

Town house with three floors: Good. Number of stairs to the top: Baaad.

The physical work was probably the least stressful part of it because I just focused and got on with it, knowing the worst thing that could happen was I'd be slightly fitter with sore hamstrings the next day. That I could handle, but leaving an empty bread bag in the cupboard when I'm hungover and I want cheese on toast! That's unforgivable.

Nights Out and City Breaks

Ha!

BE CAREFUL

I think I'm turning into a fuddy duddy. I've started saying phrases like dilly dally, dawdle, and fuddy duddy! What's happening to me? Has a dead nana possessed a part of my brain? Where this leads to worries me more. What's next? Bird watching? Chequered pyjamas? Wearing walking boots everywhere? Even while indoor food shopping!

Shudder.

I want to parent my boys safely, fairly, but when they mess about crossing the road I should shout, "Get across the road now before you get squashed by that lorry!" I guarantee that would motivate them quicker than dilly dally. Or dawdle. I see other parenting heroes dragging their kids around screaming, "Hurry up ya little shits!" but I'm like, "Hurry up my little chickens, don't dawdle." Those parents have my respect. Yeah, those kids might grow up with deep emotional scars, and some addictive tendencies, but at least they won't get ran over by a bus or use words like dawdle in public.

But that's just the tip of the iceberg. My real concern for myself and other parents is the overuse of "Be careful." I found myself telling Arlo, when he was a pre-schooler, to *be careful* carrying a glass of water. *Be careful* sitting on the stool. *Be careful* jumping off the table onto a pile of cushions. I know what the consequences of jumping from the table and missing the cushions are, but I also know how much fun it is when you get it right. I'm wondering whether there is a better way to communicate my concerns without spoiling the fun?

I began listening out for other parents and how they used it and, oh my, "Be careful" is right up there on a par with "Share." I'll delve into that one another time if I remember. "Be careful," is blurted out repeatably and without any other instructions. The kids don't even know what they're supposed to be careful of.

Children take risks in-order to understand the world around them. It's how they understand their limitations. It's their way of exploring their potential. And sometimes they're going to get hurt. And when they do, it's horrible. You want to wrap them up in love and assure them it won't happen again. Which of course we can't. It's unrealistic to suggest they'll never climb a tree again or ride a bike after falling. Or if you have kids like mine, simply walking across a room is a potential danger because coordination's the problem. I'm not going to blame the floor and carry them everywhere for the rest of their childhood. Neither would I tell myself I'm never drinking wine again after waking up rough as toast. I have a reasonable approach; I don't drink again for at least two days and I pretend all day, to The Wife, that I'm not really dying inside.

Be careful, be careful, be careful!

Is it possible to facilitate risk but minimise danger? Could you add more cushions to the pile? Yep. Practical solution. Offer them a different seat rather than a high stool? Sounds sensible. Replace glasses of water with cups? So simple. But there's another solution which I've had some success with. Rather than say "Be careful" I'm trying to highlight the potential dangers or pitfalls of their decisions in a precise way.

"Son, you do know there's water on the table? Can you see it? You might have to think about where you place your feet."

Or.

"Make sure you pick your landing spot before you jump. Have a look around the floor to make sure there's nothing in the way."

Or.

"If you're going to climb over your mum's exhausted body, make sure you use good balancing skills, Son, and try not to step on her boob."

I still want to blurt out "Be careful" at least a hundred times a day because it's so engrained. But it's definitely fading. And what really matters is the result of making this change. Are the kids hurting themselves less? Are they finding the right balance between safety and adventure? The simple answer is yes. Arlo tells me using his "Balancing skills" while walking across the top of the sofa. Even after being told for the one hundredth time, not to walk on the top of the sofa. When I set breakfast out, he'll say: "Look, Daddy, I'm using two hands," while pouring milk from the jug onto his cereal. There have been fewer accidents concerning spillages and I feel less anxious while he's exploring his surroundings.

But don't take my word for it. See how many times you hear yourself say "Be careful" in a single day. You might be surprised just how annoying you are.

FLASH NON-FICTION

The house looks nice.

Tidy.

It's 10am and no one's had a meltdown.

'I'm just gonna empty the dishwasher, Boys. Back in five.'
'Okay, Dad,' Arlo replies.

Arlo and Ove are playing so calmly with each other.

I collect the breakfast bowls and step into the kitchen.

I'm so blessed.

Screams fill the air.

I swoop back into the lounge.

Both boys are naked.

Clawing at each other's throats!

Every shelf has been emptied.

The chairs are upside down.

'What's going on?'
'He, bla, wa, na na, la, la, ra, paaaaa, heeeee!'

I return to the kitchen.

May the best beast win.

LIVING WITH TYPE 1 DIABETES

At the tender age of thirty-three, five moths before Arlo was born, I experienced what The Wife describes as an "crisis episode." For two weeks I suffered from the most severe case of dehydration, blurred vision, loss of appetite, weight loss, frequent urination (putting it mildly) and my personal favourite way to go insane, sleep deprivation. For someone who is rarely ill, my immediate and unqualified self-diagnosis was I had a bug and it would soon be on its way. Or it was brain damage, and this was my new life. And I was going to have to get used to it. Either way, like a typical bloke, I suffered in silence until it became obvious something was wrong.

My symptoms didn't ease - they persisted.

Dehydration: My mouth turned into what can only be described as polystyrene. Liquid would cascade down my chin because it struggled to penetrate the wall of cracked dryness inside my mouth. I would wake in the night short of breath because my inner cheeks and tongue were so swollen, so hard, they would clonk together like bricks. The only mild relief during these sleepless nights were the frozen pineapple chunks I sucked on regularly that managed, for a few blissful moments, to penetrate through the polystyrene, brick dust, excuse for a mouth. Just moistening my insides long enough to trick me into believing I'd gotten over the worse of it.

I basically drank anything and everything I could get my hands on. All day. But it was never enough.

Blurred vision: I've always had great eyesight. I have an exceptional left eye apparently. I'm the sort of person who can read a small sign from hundreds of feet away. I've known people (The Wife) to stand in awe at my superhero-like capabilities. But my power had gone. Everything, all the detail and clarity I usually enjoyed, was replaced with a haze like quality. Like having an unwanted switch inside my retinas and turning it to extremely drunk. I was driving to the seaside, pretending all was well, when the façade was busted.

'We come off at junction nine,' The Wife said.
'Okay, cool.'

Two minutes later.

'You were supposed to come off.'
'Oh. I couldn't see the sign.'
'What do you mean, you couldn't see the sign?'
'Erm, I've got a bit of blurred vision. But I can see all the cars.'
'What? How long have you had blurred vision?'
'I don't know, a week or two.'
'A week… right pull in at the next services. There's one coming up in a minute. Driving when you can't see the sign. Do you know how dangerous that is?'
'We've made it haven't we? Incident free.'

One minute later.

'You've just driven past the services.'
'How am I supposed to know? I can't see!'

After we swapped drivers and I spilled the beans on the situation, which in truth was a massive relief, The Wife said the words I hadn't even slightly considered.

'Sounds like Type 1 diabetes to me.'

Frequent Urination: Wow, I mean, wow! Has another human being on this planet, ever, I mean ever pissed as much as I did back then? I doubt it. And the smell, wow, oh wow. Four times during the night, hourly during the day, at one point I considered having a catheter inserted to save me the trouble of having to schedule my day around having a wee.

Sleep deprivation: A personal favourite of mine. Nothing like a little bit of sleep deprivation to force someone's mind to the edge of insanity. I've always been a light sleeper, surviving on less than most. But there's a breaking point and the worse part of the night time madness was the nightmares. As mentioned, the dehydration would often keep me awake but once I'd managed to fall asleep, I would dream about water: Craving, searching for droplets of moisture. I'd wake up panicked, clawing for the pint pot by the side of the bed and drain the contents which would usually just dribble out the sides of my mouth. Then I'd check the time and be deflated to see it was about 1am which meant I still had the rest of the night to endure.

Only one word sufficiently describes that experience, nothing fancy. . . shit. It was shit!

Loss of appetite and weight loss: I couldn't bring myself to finish a meal. Starting it was hard enough. I love cooking so preparing meals sometimes takes a couple of hours. Not a problem. It's even better with a glass of red. During this time, it was impossible to drink red wine, so in-order to build an appetite, I'd have a glass of posh organic beer. The slight fizz and earthy taste was unbelievably refreshing. Then, the anticipation would build, and my mind would communicate with my stomach and they would agree, that I was indeed starving! I would smile, present the food to The Wife and Becca, sip my beer, smile a little bit more, then watch as they tucked in. I'd look down at the plate and suddenly lose my appetite again. Back to square one.

I was desperate to feel normal again.

Once The Wife got involved the GP was contacted and an appointment was made for some blood tests. That evening I received a call from the GP's receptionist informing me not to consume *any* sugar or alcohol over the weekend and that the doctor would see me on Monday morning.

I had been drinking sugary everything because that's what I thought I needed. Which was true. Sort of. I was unable to convert the glucose into energy, so my body was using my fat supplies to keep the engine ticking over. I've always had a bit of extra chub around the mid-rift, not enough to feed a group of adults trapped in the wilderness, but definitely enough for a couple of skinny kids! But it's lucky I had a little extra meat because it meant I had something to keep me going. This may have proved to be lifesaving.

At this point in my life, I was not fully aware of the effects of carbohydrate and sugar on the blood or how it all worked. What I did know was I already had a low sugar diet, but like most, I could probably do better. So, plans were cancelled over the weekend and on Monday morning The Wife and I went to the GP to receive the unwelcome news that I had Type 1 diabetes. Life was never going to be the same again.

We sat.

He read from the computer screen.

'You have diabetes.'

The Wife and I nod our heads and hold hands.

'Type 2 diabetes.'
'Erm, what? Type 2?'

He typed out a prescription for Metformin and explained something about diet and British Olympian Steve Redgrave, and off we went to the chemist, too confused to question his knowledge.

'It's okay,' I said, 'let's play the game and see how we get on.'

The Wife wasn't convinced. And she was right.

Let me break down the next month:

The symptoms worsened.

I was unable to spend longer than half an hour on my feet.

Went back to the GP to tell him the Metformin was making me feel sick and it wasn't working. In front of two junior doctors, he said "It will take some adjustment, you'll need to get used to it."

Secretly believed I was dying.

Kidney pains started.

The Wife takes me to Accident & Emergency.

Almost immediately diagnosed with Type 1 diabetes – Insulin dependent – Type 1 diabetes.

Diagnosed after one blood test and a conversation with the hospital doctor.

Two nights in hospital, monitored hourly, insulin injections and a constant drip filled with saline to stabilise the potassium and ketone levels and bang, I felt normal again.

Two stone lighter, mentally, physically, and spiritually battered but definitely more normal.

Were we angry at the GP? The Wife was. I was relieved more than anything. That month had been a living nightmare and I was just happy to be able to sleep at night without the horrible dreams or getting up dozens of times for a wee. Once we knew it was Type 1 Diabetes, I was able to move forward and take a bit of control back from the illness. The GP had been right about the adjustment period though; figuring out the right amount of insulin to take with meals is like a game. The shittest game I've ever had the misfortune to play.

I've always been a little uncomfortable with being told it was "in the genes." That's what a specialist at the hospital said. It was in the genes and one day it had simply "switched on," and it was probably in the family. No living relatives could back up this claim but of course heritage, genes, our DNA, is all complicated stuff, and I won't deny that's a very real possibility for some people. For myself, I had a story, and after eighteen months of playing the game and getting my mind and body back into shape, I started to do some research.

An American doctor specializing in the subject had some very enlightening theories to offer and what he said fitted, precisely, with my own experience.

A week before the symptoms began and I entered the "crisis episode" fully, I injured my back while throwing a large mattress (a mattress which was hurting my back, ha-ha) at the tip. I was in agony. It took all I could muster to get in the car and drive home. The pain was unlike anything I'd experienced before and lying down on the floor, perfectly still, was the only comfort. So, I took some prescribed pain killers to alleviate my suffering. That decision was the catalyst which sparked the whole auto-immune process.

The theory.

In my early twenties I suffered with stomach ulcers due to poor diet, stress, drugs, depression etc, etc. This has been managed over the years by making better choices and improving my mental and physical health. My history of having a "leaky gut" was exacerbated by the pain killers which created a space for dairy molecules pass through the stomach wall. Once inside, an autoimmune response is triggered as your body attacks the dairy. Meanwhile the insulin producing cells of the pancreas are mistaken for the dairy molecules and the cycle begins.

This is a theory of course. But I've met people with almost exactly the same story so it's something I'm going to continue to consider and discuss.

It's a massive pain to manage, no doubt about it. When I see people munching on a piece of cake, or even just a sandwich, I think to myself, you don't know how lucky you are. After a while I got tired of having to check my blood sugar levels all the time. Thinking about it. Worrying about it. Getting it wrong and occasionally suffering from hypoglycaemia while taking care of Arlo when he was a baby. Which meant having to drink juice or eat something sugary quickly.

It's not fun.

So, I got into experimental mode and altered my diet. I eliminated certain foods for a period. I tried gluten free, plant based, paleo and several more. Most diets led back to the same place; diabetes burn out. It hits a point where I'm just exhausted thinking about it and I binge on pizza, chocolate and all the other things that make eating amazing but make managing blood sugar levels difficult.

Completely cutting foods from my diet was clearly not the way to go long term.

It's taken over six years, but I've achieved some balance. I keep the complex carbohydrates down to a minimum. I enjoy intermittent fasting and only snack when drinking alcohol. I've got used to having salad with curry, spinach instead of pasta and several other variations. Most important of all is being able to parent my boys without having a constant worry on my mind. High blood sugar on the other hand causes a lack of empathy and grumpiness, which is also something I keep an eye on as well. But occasionally, on absolute rare occasions, The Wife might suggest I need to check my blood because I'm being a bit snappy. So I do, and I can confirm with all certainty and truth, that each and every single time I'm grumpy, moody, irritable or mean, is because I have high blood sugar. 100% certainty.

CONVERSATIONS WITH A TEENAGER

I push the creaky bathroom door open. No tubs of cocoa-based products cluttering the window, blocking natural light from passing through the glass. In-fact, the shelf is clean. The bathroom's clean. Too clean.

Something's not right.

I head to the kitchen with anticipation building in my stomach.

Could this be the day?

I open the cabinet door.

It's full. Overfilled in-fact. My heart thuds against my chest as I reach for the dishwasher. It's empty. I'm... confused. This has never happened before. Becca has brought the dozen glasses and cups down from her fortress of technology, when I asked, and placed them in the dishwasher, turned it on, waited for it to finish then emptied it.

And that's on top of cleaning the bathroom.

Watery stuff fills my eyes. Maybe this is the beginning?

I'm so happy.

I win this round.

That's 5432 to Becca and 1 to me.

It's a start.

A LOCKDOWN STORY

The second lockdown is not going to be like the last one. Many lessons have been learnt but it'll be different, mainly, because we're moving to Devon. Goodbye Stockport. We've been together for nearly forty years but it's time we started seeing other towns. It's not you, it's me. Well, it's kind of you, but this is healthy. Amicable. You'll find someone who truly appreciates you I'm sure.

We can thank the lockdowns for this change. It helped The Wife and I to revaluate. We had the time and space to work through several issues and come out the other side feeling fresh. We had a plan. It wasn't plain sailing though. Things had to get a bit messy before they got better. From the end of March 2020 to the beginning of June 2020, we were stuck in a cycle. Asking the same questions each day: "What day is it?" "How many snacks do you think we've had?" "When was the last time I showered?"

It became a habit to open wine with lunch, pretty much every day.

"Well it's 7pm somewhere, hahahahah."

And there was the boredom to contend with.

Wandering around the same streets over and over again, searching for some secret space, a strange tree, an unknown park, anything to break the monotony of lockdown. Anything that offered sanctuary from the mental and physical strain of lockdown with small children. For an hour. Five minutes. Any amount of time! Just a moment to watch my boys play independently without them asking me questions about the complexities of the human psyche, or about Peppa Pig's continual promotion of gender stereotypes. Or more relaxed topics like what is electricity made of? Or why does poo stink? Usually, I'm more than happy to answer any questions the boys throw at me. I love playing and I absolutely know the importance and benefits of the great outdoors but halfway through the first lockdown 2020, I just couldn't be bothered anymore.

'We need to get them out for a bit,' The Wife nudged me between the ribs.
'I don't want to do anything.' I felt nothing. 'I'm too bored to move.'
'There's a post on Facebook about some fairy doors that have been put up around the streets,' she informed me.
'You're trying to tempt me off the settee with fairy doors? Ha.'
'The boys neeeeed to get out, they're doing my head in.'

I scraped my chin against the shards of delicious sea salted crisps sprinkled around my chest and neck, away from the *Buy 12 bottles of wine, delivered to your house within the hour* advertisement on my phone, towards The Wife's bloodshot teary eyes that were staring into my soul. Pleading with me to do something with the boys.

'What time is it?'
'The clock is right there,' she pointed with her annoyed head.
'Hmmpff.'

I scraped my chin back the other way towards the silver clock hanging on the wall. Tick tocking away. I'd never noticed before, but it was suddenly the loudest clock I'd ever heard. So ridiculously loud it hurt my ears. How had I never noticed before? Not sure why.

God I was so bored. I Just needed to get up and go look at the damn fairy doors!

A burst of energy surged into my legs and arms, sent from a part of my brain which wants to support The Wife and recognises her cry for help. I saw the solution clearly in my mind's eye but, as quickly as it came, it went.

'It's half eleven,' I told her.
'So?'
'It's lunch time.'
'It won't hurt you all to miss a meal.'
'I'm not going to rise to that comment.'

I zoned out again and continued with a very important task which was happening beneath my grubby t-shirt. I didn't need to look at The Wife to know the expression on her face. I could feel it like a cold drip down my spine. I removed my hand to reveal a greyish, bluey, brownish piece of belly button fluff wrapped in black hairs which I held high in the air.

'Look at the size of that,' I marvelled.

The Wife pressed a hand to her throat.

'You're disgusting. What's wrong with you?'

I held it higher.

'This is a record breaker.'

Higher!

'Have you ever seen a piece of belly button fluff as big as that?'
'You need help.'
'Ha ha. I know why. Ha ha, I know why.'
'Why?' she asks, suddenly interested.

Even though I was talking about belly button fluff she couldn't help herself. Forever the inquisitive type. A lifelong learner. It's in her nature.

'I've been wearing this t-shirt day and night for five days straight. No shower, plus it's a new t-shirt which has never been washed, plus wearing it 24/7, plus having a really hairy belly button equals this masterpiece. It's a natural consequence. It's science. This should be named after me, like a new star. Put in a London museum next to that blob of fat they found in the sewer.'
'What are you on about?'
'I am... the Lint Collector.'

For reasons beyond my knowledge, she didn't share my enthusiasm. Each quarter of her face seemed to point in different directions and twitched simultaneously. I was afraid.

'I'll get the kid's coats,' I said, peeling myself off the settee.
'I think that's for the best,' The Wife spoke through gritted teeth.

THE CYCLE OF NO

It took a while before it became a conscious thing for me. This *cycle of no*. I'd observed The Wife doing it for years with a lot of success. No matter how much they screamed or cried, she never caved. It was a sight to behold. Completely stone cold. I felt it was a bit dictatory if I'm honest, but she lets me go to the pub and occasionally play with her boobs, so I've never questioned this totalitarian regime.

'Mum, can I have a snack?'
'No.'
'Mum, can we watch a film?'
'No.'
'Mum, can I have a drink of water.'
'No.'
'Mum, have you got a plaster?'
'No.'

She made it look so easy. The pure no-ness of it all. How did she do it so devoid of emotion? So detached? It was amazing. I'm not cut from the same cloth, you see. I'm still wearing L plates whereas she's been a mum for about fifteen years longer than me. Many of the parenting pitfalls I come across she's already navigated. Oh, and how she likes to let me know that at every opportunity.

'I'm going to let them stay up late and watch another film,' I say. Bursting with enthusiasm.
'Hmm mm.'
'What?'
'Nothing.'
'I know that face.'
'What face?'
'That face.'
'I don't know what to tell you.'

Pause for effect.

'But if you let them stay up late it'll be a nightmare getting them to sleep. They'll be overtired and full of sugar. They'll turn nasty and it'll end in tears,' she tells me.
'How can they turn nasty watching Toy Story?'
'Hmm mm.'
'I'll deal with them.'
'I know you will.'

An hour later.

'Say it.'
'No.'
'Say… it.'
'You were right okay. You were right. They're horrible ungrateful beasts.'

I'm soft. I see that. I have faith everything will be okay in the end if you just give them what they want. Or at least make a deal. I know it's ridiculous, but I think I know why. I got a lot of nos as a child. There was no negotiation. You had the right to storm off in a mood but there was no point arguing about it. I want the scales to tip more to the yes rather than the nos. Mainly because I want an easy life but also because the things they ask for, overall, aren't unreasonable.

'Dad, can we go to the park?'
'Yes.'
'Dad, can we play little dragons?'
'Yes.'
'Dad, has mum always been your boss?'
'Yes – no. We're a team, Son.'
'Ha ha. Whatever.'

I've been a stay-at-home parent a few times while The Wife has pursued her career interests, so I've had to develop some parenting techniques that don't involve using a super deep authoritarian voice or putting a symbolic foot down! I'm all about physical play. Dens, sword fighting, wrestling, repetitive games of hide and seek over and over again, anything to keep them from realising I'm just filling time before mum returns and I can chill. I like a smooth ride.

'Dad, can we have a snack?'
'It's nearly lunch time, can't you wait?'
'No.'
'Okay, I tried. Here you go lovely boy.'

Good old-fashioned misdirection worked for ages when they were toddlers. They asked for a snack, I showed them a balloon, and they forget what they'd asked for. Bubbles were very effective. Lion King was an absolute winner. But techniques like that only last so long. Eventually you need to bend down to spitting level and try and reason with the little beasts. Of course, they can't have everything they want but my boys are skilled at convincing me I'm wrong. That I'm the one being unfair.

They are relentless in the pursuit of the things they want. The screaming and shouting over a rubbish milk biscuit that tastes like sand is truly remarkable. I start to question my sanity. They've had cereal, fruit, toast, crackers, more fruit, water, juice, an ice lolly, a cheese sandwich with cucumber and crisps, more fruit and it's not even lunchtime. And here they are again, kicking off over a flipping sand biscuit to the point of turning red and getting sweaty. What am I supposed to think? That they would cause such a fuss because of some invisible need to be in control over their own lives or something?

Crazy teacher talk!

That was the old me. I beat him to a bloody pulp and placed him in a large box in my subconscious with the guy that thinks you must iron both sides of a t-shirt. I know how to access the *cycle of no* now. One day it just happened. Something snapped.

'Dad, can we watch another film?'
'Ye… no.'

Both boys stopped chewing and looked up from their feeding buckets.

'Ahem… I said no.'

Ove kicked his small wooden table to one side. His feeding bucket and organic bamboo cup hit the laminate floor. There was a small spillage. Nothing I couldn't handle. He leaned forward off the wooden chair, which fits perfectly under his wooden table (it's a set) and began to lift his food splattered naked body up with the intention of kicking off big time.

Arlo. Without taking his eyes from the organic bamboo cup of juice raised and resting two inches away from his mouth in his left hand, cool as anything, placed his loving right hand onto his brothers heaving chest.

'I got this,' Arlo told his brother.

He took a sip from the cup then passed it to Ove who finished it in one, wiped his mouth with the back of his hand then threw the cup over his shoulder, adding it to the rest of the mess on the floor. Arlo patted his chest once more and Ove sat down.

Arlo looked at me for the first time since I dared to utter that forsaken word.

'See that mess there?' Arlo pointed with his chubby thumb. 'That's nothing.'
'I'm well-aware of your capabilities, Son.'
'So why do it to yourself, DAD?'
'Dad now is it? What happened to Daddy?'

He removed the dented top hat he'd been wearing since dawn and placed it on the slightly bigger wooden table in front of him. He brushed crumbs and unidentified sticky objects off his underpants then licked his finger – grimaced slightly then did it again. He stood up off the sofa with the physicality of a boss having to deal with the incompetence of his staff for the hundredth time that day.

'I'm guessing, because we've watched three films already, you think it's about time we turn it off. Maybe do some colouring? A bit of home learning? Let me guess, you want to do some baking?'

I looked through the doorway into the kitchen where I'd already organised the ingredients for carrot and walnut muffins.

'I bet you've already separated the ingredients into bowls,' Arlo said.

He looked sick of the predictability of it all.

'I… er.'
'let me tell you how this is gonna go,' Arlo stepped towards me pointing at the doorway to the kitchen. 'You're going to go in there and bake those muffins. If mum asks later, I'll say we all did it

together, if that makes things easier on you. You'll say we can only have one muffin' but we'll have at least three.'

He smirked and clapped his hands together real slow and deliberate.

'Mum will be like, "You're such a good Daddy," and we'll be like, "He's the best." Then mum will say, "Why don't you have a glass of wine? I'll put the kids to bed." Doesn't that sound perfect?'
'You think you know me so well.'
'You never know, she might even say, "Why don't you go to the pub for a few beers, Babe?" Doesn't that sound even better?'
'I've thought of an alternative actually.'
'You have?'

He used the end of a toy dragon to pick food from in-between his teeth. He inspected the scrap of flesh on the dragon's tail then put it into his mouth and swallowed. He nodded his head, ready to negotiate. The dragon flew across the room and landed in a basket below the window near where I stood.

'Go on,' Arlo said.
'Picture this scene,' I said stepping towards him. 'Mum comes home, and the place is a wreck. I'm a wreck. Close to tears. "The boys have been awful, Babe. I don't know what's wrong with them," I'll say. She'll hug me tight. Kiss my cheek. "I didn't have time to clean up or make any tea, Babe. I'm sorry." I'll tell her.'
'You wouldn't do that?'
'I wouldn't do that you say. You know how much mum looks forward to one of my nice teas after a busy day don't you?'
'She loves it.'
'How about this, "I can't cope, Babe. Maybe I should get a full-time job and we'll pay for childcare? Or maybe you should go part time and have them?"'
'You couldn't handle a full-time job anymore.'
'Couldn't I?'

We stared into each other's soul.

'You won't pay for other people to bring up your kids. You say that all the time.'
'Wouldn't I?'

I had him on the ropes and he knew it.

'One more film then we'll…'
'No!'

That time I said it so clearly. With confidence. It's biblical. I knew I meant it that time and so did they.

'Noooo.'

Ove fell back off his chair and thrashed and wriggled on the floor like he was searching for a hot piece of coal on his skin. Arlo stumbled back to the sofa, weak at the knees, weak in the gut!

'We're going to clean up this mess. Turn the telly off. Bake the muffins and then go for a walk. Okay?'

They didn't answer. They didn't need too. I had experienced a parenting revolution. I had entered into… the *cycle of no!*

Baby Wearing's Cool

'Here we go again,' I said.
'Trust me, all the cool dads wear them.'
'Where? Who?'
'Chorlton dads.'
'We don't live in Chorlton.'
'You could bring the cool to Stockport?'
'You do realise, only a massive nerd would ever say something like that?'

The Wife has a habit of trying to lure me into doing something a little alternative by placing the word cool somewhere in the conversation. I don't know why she bothers. I already know I am. How? I smoke roll up cigs with liquorice skins when on the wine. I wear a flat cap. I don't watch football and I do the ironing! That's pretty-cool, right?

'Will you try?' She continued.

I looked down at the multicoloured stretchy thing in her hand. This was going to be a defining moment in my life as a dad. A line in the sand. Once stepped over there was going to be no way back. The Wife was going to start talking to me about this stuff all the time. Try to *include* me. Make me go places and talk to people I have zero interest in. But this meant a lot to her. I could tell by the way she looked at me with this *don't you want to have a shared interest* bollocks.

'Sure, why not?'
'Yay.'

In case you have no idea what a stretchy is, I'm talking about slings. Carriers. Baby wearing. And if you have considered giving it a go, but for whatever reason you're resistant, which I totally get because if like me you thought you'd look like an idiot, I'm just going to admit it right now, it's great. I love it! Not a big fan of talking about it excessively like The Wife and her slingy mums do. It's verging on a cult if I'm truthful. They gather in large groups inside small church halls and fill tables with every type of baby wearing paraphernalia in existence. The vicars stay well out the way as these women, drenched in hormones and lavender, sway to some distant drum beat from one side of the room to another with their babies, or toddlers, latched onto their milky boobs. They advise and congratulate each other on the suitability of their chosen sling or carrier, while reminding each other how the slings won't depreciate in value. *It's safer than investing in gold* I overheard one of them say while munching on a mound of chocolate cake and tandem wearing her ginormous twins.

I'm telling you now, don't fall for it. One that costs forty pound can be just as comfortable as one handmade by Mother Teresa's great granddaughter which costs more than a family holiday to Ibiza oldtown.

As a babywearing dad, I'm fussed over something frantic when I arrive. And I love it. Crafty hands all over the place. Pulling, grabbing, and flattening parts of my body ensuring Arlo is secure. The Wife has no problem with it because it's all in the name of baby wearing. But having a cool dad on board is not the top prize of the day oh no. I'm pushed to the side like a half-chewed chicken leg when a fresh-faced new mum barges in through the heavy double doors with a high-tech John Lewis pushchair worth more than my car. The slingy mums release a collective sigh, dish whoever, or whatever they were doing, and head straight towards the new mum. All comradery's out the window as they push and hustle for position to see who is going to match this newbie with the right baby wearing solution.

The new mum doesn't stand a chance. In a whirlwind of colour and cake she's quietly separated from her brand-new pushchair which gets parked in the far corner of the hall with the rest of them. The dusty relics destined to rest amongst their own kind until the end of time. Sad and yet beautiful like a great elephant graveyard. Sacred and not to be disturbed. The new mum might leave one high-tech pushchair short but her initiation into the cult is complete once her crying baby settles inside the woven sling expertly wrapped by several of her new kin.

'My baby's stopped crying,' Newbie says.
'Hmm mm,' her new sisters reply.
'But she never stops.'
'Hmm mm. You're one of us now.'

I love wearing Arlo. We look damn cute together. And we certainly don't get bored of all the attention we get while out and about. I had no idea of the pulling power of having a kid. Pulling power might be laying it on a bit thick though. It's mainly nanas and grannies stopping us but we love it anyway!

'Isn't he gorgeous,' random granny will say.
'Don't call me that, he gets jealous,' I reply.

Wink, wink, nudge, nudge. How we laugh!

Besides from all that, baby wearing's about the closeness. Bonding with your baby. I quickly moved away from stretchy woven slings and such like and found a carrier with buckles on the straps which were easy for me to handle. Slings were designed for people with a dexterity beyond my skill level.

Useful points to consider if you're not sure:

- Your hands are free so you can make breakfast, dinner, and tea.
- And wash the pots, hoover, and generally tidy the house, while mum eats cake.
- Your hands are free to carry your partner's shopping bags around town.
- Babies love it in the sling. It calms them down when they're having a meltdown.
- The sling does for the man what being a mum does for a mum. Sort of.
- Your hands are free to make the cake while your partner tells you about a sling that she wants.
- You and the baby feel closer.

If you'd have told me a few years ago I'd be talking about baby wearing, in any way shape or form, I would have said you were high. The truth is, I felt like a bit of a spare part when Arlo was born. The Wife was his everything and my role was more about supporting her. Which, of course, is fine but it was difficult to know my place as far as the baby was concerned. He wasn't really soothed by my touch and I couldn't feed him because my stupid nipples didn't do anything! Baby wearing helped me feel closer to him while not really needing to try very hard. I'm not suggesting baby wearing's the best or only way to go. It worked for me and any future dads able to try it out should give it go. What's the worst that could happen? Getting a bit of attention from a silver lady? You can handle it.

CONVERSATIONS WITH THE WIFE

'Here we go again.'
'Don't be like that.'
'I've just painted the banister.'
'We've got new flooring too.'
'I'd forgotten about that.'

She pours me a glass of red and passes it to me.

'It doesn't matter about those things.'
'Easy for you to say, I do the work.'
'You like doing it though.'
'I do have other interests you know?'
'Like what?'
'I was thinking of doing a night course.'
'In what?'
'Erm… horticulture.'
'Rubbish.'

I sip my delicious wine. She's got this all planned to a T.

'The thought of dismantling the wardrobes. Boxing everything up.'

'What about it?'

'Classic you. You only see the results not the work that needs doing.'

'I just get in the way. Better to just leave you to it.'

She empties my favourite lightly sea salted crisps into a bowl. I take one. Tasty!

'It's not a problem to be honest.'

'Sorted then. I'll let them know.'

'Hang on. Don't you think we need to talk about a few other issues first?'

'Like what?'

'Like what? … like moving to the other end of the country and house swapping with strangers.'

'We've done it before.'

'Not to the other end of the country we haven't.'

'And with no support.'

'You're not selling this.'

'We don't have much support now.'

I sip my wine and munch my crisps.

'Plymouth is near Cornwall, yeah?'

'Next door.'

'I've always wanted to go down there.'

'Exactly.'

'Can we really be bothered moving the boys again?'

'I didn't say it would be straight forward.'

'Do they have any Beach Schools?'

'All sorts.'

'Near the house?'

'Uh huh.'

She sips her wine and nibbles a large crisp.

'How far from the house?'

'Not that far.'

'How far?'
'About half an hour.'
'On foot?'
'In the car.'
'Too far.'
'It might be a quick half an hour.'
'Ha ha. You really believe that don't you?'
'They don't have to go every day. '
'That's true.'
'We don't need to work every day either.'
'I like that.'
'The rent is half.'
'Now I'm listening.'
'So that's settled.'
'Chill.'

I switch the telly on and sit back.

'I'm not rushing into a decision.'
'We need to decide ASAP.'
'Why?'
'There's a deadline for the other family to get their kids into grammar school.'
'Did they tell you that?'
'Yep.'
'So, they're serious then?'
'Very.'
'Can we be bothered?'
'It'll be like living on holiday.'
'Now you're talking.'
'Beach every week.'
'Every week?'
'Every day.'
'We could get a dog?'

I knew there was more to this.

'No way.'
'Why?'
'Honestly?'
'Yeah, why?'
'I can't be bothered picking the shit up.'
'Arrr.'
'I see people picking shit up and I just think, nah, you're a slave.'
'I agree. No dog.'
'Defo need wetsuits though. Fancy a bit of wild swimming.'
'We could get a boat.'
'Like a canoe?'
'A sailboat.'
'Piss off.'

TALKING TO STRANGERS

There are many sayings from childhood that spring to mind now I'm the parent.

"Wash behind your ears or spuds will grow there."

Classic.

"Don't pick your nose - your head will cave in."

Used by every teacher at my primary school throughout the 1980s.

I guess they're supposed to be fun, yet I can't help but think that at the core they instil a sense of fear within a child's easily coerced mind. You know, back from the good old days when children were to be "seen and not heard," and it was the norm to give your kids a good smack now and again. For their own good, of course. Knowing Arlo as I do, he thinks very literally and if I said his head will cave in if he picks his nose, I reckon he'll be discussing it in therapy for most of his adult life.

What we really want is for children, anyone, to not pick their nose while you're trying to have a civil conversation with them.

'Can you stop doing that while we're talking please?'
'Wait a second, neeearly got it.'

Once the rooting is complete, the picker is faced with that universal decision; whether to wipe it on the furniture or roll it into a ball and flick it across the room or, option three, a popular choice with kids, eat it! I've witnessed a few bloody noses as a result of over enthusiastic rooting - suffered a few myself - and I've seen some humongous bogeys balanced on the end of proud fingers, but I have never, not once, seen a child's head implode while doing it. Or heard of it happening to anyone.

'Good morning, children,' The headteacher says.
'Goooood mooooorning, Miss.'
'I have some terrible news. We've been informed that Steven Parkes from year 4, who was caught picking his nose yesterday while queuing for lunch, later suffered from a collapsed head. His parents said he's now three inches smaller. Let this be a lesson to you all!'

Never happened.

And spuds behind the ear! Don't get me started. I remember checking while in the bath, convinced I must have some. It's hard to connect with the distant memory but the residue of confusion was very clear. The last thing I would have thought of doing back then was ask someone if it was true or not. Oh no. Much better to allow the thoughts to rattle around inside my brain, unchallenged, able to mutate into something much worse.

I don't want my boys to be confused about their bodies.

Or the multi-verse either!

I remember lying on my Nana's sheep skin rug when I was about eight, and from nowhere I was struck suddenly by one of those uncontrollable shivers that moves through your whole body. I'm eight, so I don't give it much thought. You just accept it as another one of them weird body things no one talks about; like constipation and that crusty bit in your eye unhelpfully referred to as "sleep."

I shivered. I accepted. I moved on.

Then…

'That's someone walking over your grave,' Nana said.

Mind blown!

I was watching *H.R. Pufnstuf* on VHS at the time, which was weird enough, but this was next level. I don't think a week passes without reliving that moment and linking it to my childhood curiosity of the supernatural and all things weird. Was someone walking over my grave in the *past* or the *future*? Was my Nana a time traveller? Why was someone walking over my grave anyway? Have they no respect for the dead?

My life was never the same.

Some sayings were actually quite sensible. More like instructions.

"Stop, Look, Listen and Think."

A lifesaving instruction that was drilled into us and for good reason. But I think there's one saying which trumps them all. It was blasted into my impressionable young mind from all directions by family members and teachers alike:

"Don't talk to strangers."

Right. I get it. I understand why this was promoted so fiercely. The world can be harsh. Dangerous. We know there are people out there capable of hurting children. History shows us what they are capable of. The horrific Moors murders of the 1960's were probably still fresh in the minds of the adults of the 1980's, which meant they were very aware of the potential dangers out there. Then in 1990 two boys abducted a toddler and the world was faced with some scary truths; suddenly, children weren't even safe from their own. Strangers weren't just men and women trying to entice little ones into cars with sweets anymore. Danger was everywhere.

"Don't talk to strangers," had never been more vital.

Scary times.

But, for me and my boys in the here and now, our days are significantly brightened by our interactions with strangers. I talk to strangers every day. Random grandads outside the supermarket. A nana on the bus. Other parents at the park or library. My boys see this and know that it's natural to interact with others.

When we enter Stockport library, I let my boys explore. I allow a little feral. Controlled feral. Not pushing all the books off the shelves feral. There are spinning chairs in the middle of the main area and they're lots of fun to sit on and use for imaginative play. The bookcases are perfect for playing hide and seek and chase. You're probably reading this and thinking it doesn't sound like suitable behaviour for a library… and you're absolutely right. Will not argue with you on that one.

Most of the people in there tap away on keyboards, read books, and generally just ignore my kids or others with similar feral plans. Sometimes parents, like me, who are trying to offer their children freedom while respecting the right of other users to not be dribbled on or disturbed, will gravitate towards each other, discuss their feral kids, and play the who's-had-less-sleep game. I always win.

There are so many social issues to consider while interacting with new people. I have an appreciation for a person's personal space and their right to be left alone. There are social anxieties, cultural differences and a vast array of other reasons why a stranger may not want to interact with you or your touchy-feely kids. I explain to both boys the importance of understanding personal boundaries and how to judge through people's facial expressions and body language whether they want to interact or not. They don't always get it right but I try and stay alert to their movements so I can jump in before Ove climbs up on some random guy's knee and starts rewording his emails on the library computer!

But how can they learn to relate to strangers and navigate tricky social interactions without the opportunity to practice and engage? They can't, can they? There's risk involved of course. Allowing them to push the boundaries may result in them receiving a telling off from someone. The interaction would then present an opportunity to explain to the boys about what had happened, how it had escalated, and how it could be avoided in the future.

And I'm sure they'd nod, pretend to understand, then do it again five minutes later.

We want to keep our children safe. But in the same breath, we don't hide all the knives in the kitchen or put armbands on them each time we visit a park to feed the ducks. A spot of common sense is required me thinks. Instead of saying don't talk to stranger, we tell our boys to never go **anywhere,** with **anyone,** without letting us know first. We've told Arlo, as gently as possible, that not everyone you meet is a good person. We've discussed characters in films who enjoy hurting children or animals (Cruella De Vil is a good example) and this helped to give a little context to the conversation.

There is a saying that sprung to mind recently. Something I have extensive knowledge of. Ever heard the one about playing with your willy too much? That it'll drop off! Guess what? Mine's still fully attached, and I've been playing with it for years. I am genuinely concerned for Arlo's well-being though. If he continues tugging on his, with an enthusiasm I've never witnessed before, he could be the first to lose it.

'Dad. It came off.'
'I didn't think it was possible, Son. But you proved me wrong.'
'What am I going to do now?'
'You're going to stop picking your nose for a start.'

FUCK OFF, GLUE EAR

There's no doubt about it, I suspected life would change significantly when I became a parent. The Wife had gently, over several months, informed me that I'd have to alter some of my personal habits, rituals or quirks, as I like to call them.

- Stop drinking alcohol every night – Tick. No problem.
- No recreational drugs (on weeknights) – Pfff, done!
- The house can't be tidy all the time – We'll see about that Mrs.
- Control my youthful urges – Erm… why?

I'm a smart man - *got me a degree and everything* - so I also knew there'd be some additions to my already jam-packed modern man chores.

- Learn a million new skills I was not previously equipped to manage – On going.
- Be more sensitive, learn to cry again, explore and share my feelings – Smashed it!
- Put the baby to bed – Erm… Nope.

Why? Our babies have no interest, what-so-ever, of being put to bed by me or anyone else except The Wife. And even then, it's tricky. It all started with Arlo. If The Wife had the audacity to peel herself away from him when he was a baby, maybe to get a drink, maybe to treat herself to a nice long wee that wasn't cut off mid-stream, he would sense the milky nipple had been removed from his immediate vicinity and wake up screaming. If she even thought about sneaking downstairs to devour a packet of biscuits, no way mama! He would scream the house down.

She might have reached the bedroom door, slid her dressing gown off the hook, eased it slowly onto her tired shoulders - feeling confident, or naïve, she may have taken one final look behind her, just to check if he was asleep, and he'd be sat up straight, questioning with his watery eyes, "Where the hell do you fink you're going with my supper? Get back to bed now!"

We were completely at a loss at what to do. Not aided by unhelpful suggestions to leave him to scream it out of his system, or doctors who said he'd grow out of it. It was a lonely place to be. Was it night terrors? Past life regression? We tried Reiki, and a Cranial Osteopath. We went gluten free god-dam-it! We hired the Native American guy from the *Poltergeist* film to check if the house was buried on an ancient burial ground, but even he'd never seen a child scream so violently, and with so much dribble. He just threw the burning sage onto the floor and jumped headfirst through the bedroom window, never to be seen again.

Nothing worked.

Sleep deprivation causes many things. None of them fun. Anxiety. Mood swings. Lack of empathy... and, erm... probably something to do with short term memory loss but I forgot! Have you ever experienced a come down from amphetamine? It was like that but without the good bit first where you clean the house and feel thin. We began anticipating the screams. Our ridged bodies filled with anxiety because being woken from REM sleep to the horror of our reality every fifty minutes was worse than pre-empting it and trying to soothe him before it escalated. Which, of course, meant never sleeping.

After two and a half years, The Wife read an article online about children misdiagnosed with ADHD when in-fact they were suffering with glue ear: Delayed speech, mouth breathers, unbelievable amounts of dribble and mood swings. The list went on and Arlo hit every point on it. This knowledge was the catalyst for change. We had to harass our GP for a referral to the ENT department. Pumping him full of pain killers helped but having grommets in both ears and the adenoid from behind his nose removed was the real game changer. Life got significantly better for all of us after that. Not perfect by any means but we started to get at least four hours on the bounce and that was flipping amazing.

Then Ove began exhibiting all the same symptoms as Arlo had. We couldn't believe it. At this point I won't lie, I felt sorry for us the parents, not the kids. But at least we knew what to look out for, so we were right on it! We weren't going to take no for an answer from the doctors this time.

I'm one of those types of people who asks "why" quite a lot. I'm a bit crazy like that. Why do children get glue ear? Why does the adenoid become enlarged? In our experience with health professionals, no one really cares and when you try and talk about it, you get nowhere.

'Why isn't there more focus on prevention rather than dealing with the symptoms?' I asked.

The Specialist looked at The Wife. The Wife looked at me.

'It's a valid question? I mean, it would prevent a lot of pain and anguish for all involved. Especially the kids.'

The Specialist placed a pen down and faced The Wife. Ignoring me.

'Mrs Glennon. Don't bring your husband again. He's annoying.'

Both boys had the procedures within a couple of months of one another. It made a massive difference to our family, but we'd co-slept from the beginning and somehow the boys needed to understand we no longer wanted their sweaty bodies anywhere near us during the night. A new routine was required. A new bunkbed and a watertight plan. 5pm teatime. 05:30pm bath. 06:00pm till 7pm low lights and chilled music. Calm games. Ove could have a bottle of oat milk, stories read, wees had, complex questions concerning the nature of Cheerio's resolved. One parent kissed and squeezed. Two children in bed with classical music tinkering away, night light on and voila! It only went and flipping worked! Kind of. Mostly. For a while. Getting them to sleep is a doddle now but getting them to stay asleep continues to be a massive pain in the arse.

Why Do They Always Shout?

'DAD, CAN YOU PLAY WITH ME?'

I glance at myself in the mirror: Pen on my face, questionable stains all over my t-shirt, tired red eyes, one sock. I'm stood up but I can't feel my legs. I was on the way to the kitchen for something, I think, but I have no idea what for.

'COME ON, DAD. LET'S PLAY CARS.'

I'm holding a small fire engine. There're dozens of cars all around me on the floor like a minefield. There're homemade ramps leaning against every piece of furniture. Sections of wooden train track, which I was sure had been sent to the charity shop but is now scattered in all directions.

Confusion.

'Haven't we been playing cars for the last... erm, is it daytime yet?'

'I WANNA WATCH SECRET LIFE OF PETS.'

'You just said you wanted to –'

'COME ON, DAD, LET'S WATCH SECRET LIFE OF PETS TWO.'

Why is he shouting at me? He's about half a metre away, stood on The Wife's exhausted body, giving him a few extra inches in height and sound range, naked and splattered with everything.

'Son, use your indoor voice, please.'

'I WANT SOMETHING TO EAT. GET ME SOMETHING.'

'Hmm, mmm, arrr, oooh.'

'What's that, Babe?'

The Wife pulls Chase from Paw Patrol, who looks like he's been mentally and physically abused, off her face.

'I said, why's he always shouting?'

'MUMMY! THERE YOU ARE. I COULDN'T FIND YOU.'

'I think there's something wrong with him,' I say.

'I WANNA WATCH SECRET LIFE OF PETS TWO.'

'I heard you, Son. Please stop shouting, you're gonna wake your brother up,' The Wife says.

There's a sudden thud above us. The Wife and I look up. Dust detaches itself from the light fitting and drifts along a beam of sunlight towards the crack in the curtain.

THUD THUD THUD down the stairs.

We stare at the door.

It opens. Slowly.

'MAMAAAAA,' Ove screams.

NOW THERE'S TWO OF THEM!

The wild toddler with piecing blue eyes sniffs the air. He smells the last traces of milk inside The Wife's boob. He licks his lips. I've seen that look before. He won't be satisfied until he's drained her completely.

'MAMAAAAA.'

I crash through the minefield of cars, tracks, and ramps, then army roll forward. I place Chase back on The Wife's face, muffling out the groans, then collect Arlo under one arm as I jump towards the dribbling toddler in the doorway, cutting off his boob attack before he formulates a plan of action. I kick the kitchen door open and enter. A third arm smashes through my ribcage splattering the worktop with pieces of bone and dressing gown. This new arm instinctively knows what to do and stuffs chocolates, biscuits, and cartons of juice into their hands and into my pockets. I kick kitchen door again and head for the stairs.

'WHERE'S MY IPAD? I WANNA WATCH-'

He calls it an iPad but it's an Amazon Fire Tablet, but there's no point telling him that. He doesn't care! I throw them both up the stairs with the exact amount of force required for a gentle landing then return to the kitchen.

'Where are they, where are they?'
'MAMAAAA.'
'WHERE'S MY IPAD?'

The tablets are charging next to the toaster. I plugged them in last night.

'God is great!'

I grab the tablets off the side while my third arm unplugs them from their chargers, and I run. I run like I've never run before. The world is just a blur. My feet don't touch the floor. There is no floor. No time or space. My body ascends to a higher vibrational state where matter doesn't exist. Again, my third arm works independently, interpreting my thoughts without hesitation and grabs my *Game of Thrones* novel out of my coat pocket which hangs from the banister, I ain't watching *Secret Life of Pets* again! No, no, no, and I ascend the stairs towards the boys who are regrouping their forces.

Not today boys!

In a flash we're in their bedroom with our backs to the wall, duvets on our legs, tablets in hands, snacks in mouths.

'Today, you can watch all the films.'
'ALL THE FILMS?'
'Yes. And eat all the snacks.'
'ALL OF THEM?'
'Yes, all of them.'
'YAY,' they shout.

They always shout.

A LOCKDOWN STORY

Lockdown has altered my perception of time, maaan. I have no idea what day it is. There's nothing concrete left in the world which says, today is Friday, today is the day I drink wine and eat crisps, because this is everyday now. I don't need to wait until Friday because there is no Saturday! Do you know what I mean? When I was a kid we bathed on a Sunday because school was the next day. As an adult I showered after a day's work because it's what you do. It's routine. Unconscious routine. But there is no school. NO work. Only wine and crisps. And the kids, of course, but I haven't seen them for ages. They've blended into the sofa. They're one. I just throw food in the general direction of the sofa, the cushions flap wildly for a few seconds then it all calms down again and I return every so often to clean the scraps up off the floor.

I presume they're okay. The sofa hasn't told me any different.

It's an alternative reality, you see. Where all the rules and structures that usually keep me balanced in life have vanished. Have you ever thought, *I wish I could spend more time with my family?* No problem, mate. In this reality your family is here, all the time. There are not many places you can go anymore. Once you've visited the same boring park over and over again, you eventually decide outside bad, inside good.

Everything you've ever wanted, sort of, is right here for you. A nice man delivers boxes of wine straight to your door. You play this really funny game where you put six bottles in the garage - they're for Christmas - and you put the other six in the kitchen - they're for the week ahead. The first six don't last long and the other six never judge when you appear at the garage door.

'I thought Christmas was a little ambitious if I'm honest,' Garage Wine says.
'Thanks for saying that.'
'Why don't you have a bottle with lunch?'
'What a wonderful idea.'

Just admit now, wine is better than water.

You get on first name terms with hundreds of Amazon delivery drivers. They don't need to rush anymore. Everyone's in the house watching the brand-new Disney Plus subscription.

'Just leave it next to the bins if I'm not in, Alex,' you say for a laugh.

Alex smiles politely because he's heard it about twenty times already that morning and it wasn't funny the first time. He knows you aren't going anywhere. The Amazon drivers are living their best life and it would be even better if they could just shove it through your window and move on without having to listen to the drunken ramblings of all the parents desperate for a bit of adult conversation.

The supermarket trucks are the only other vehicles on the road. Those drivers don't have time to chat because they're so overwhelmed with orders. They supply large nets that you erect near your front door and they throw the shopping from the back of the trucks into it. And that's okay because in this reality you're a lazy slob and you don't want to come face-to-face with the person who's delivering your junk food and booze while you're wearing a dressing gown which looks like it was found in a skip.

Seriously, when was the last time I showered?

I have no idea, but I'm convinced that after a while, once my nose doesn't recognise the stench as an issue any longer, imagine an out-of-date tin of corned beef mixed with a dash of garlic, a dollop of vinegar and a whole lot of parmesan cheese, revolting to you, maybe? But to me, it evolves into something quite pleasant. Kind of homely. Like homemade bread mixed with something earthy.

The Wife's not said anything. And she's got a very sensitive nose, plus the inability to disguise the look of disgust on her face, so I must be on to something here? Smell is subjective though isn't it? A fine example: I was ironing recently, and I thought to myself, this new washing powder's a bit funky. In fact, it's not very nice at all. But I carried on. The Wife likes to add white vinegar to everything, so I never know what is normal anymore. But one second after entering the room, The Wife says, "Cat piss?" And she was right. Once she pointed it out, I was like, oh yeah. But she's said nothing about my new body odour so I'm going to continue with my homemade bready earthiness until things are back to normal. When Friday is for drinking wine and eating crisps, and Sunday is for having a bath!

BECCA

It took me a while to figure it out, but you know what's harder than being a stepdad? Being a stepdaughter! I'm sorry it took so long to understand this. Probably could have made your life a bit easier in parts if I'd have known it sooner. This is not an excuse but you need to know, to understand, that I was wildly unprepared for parenthood, in any form, when I was 29 years old. I liked the simple things in life: going out drinking, having zero responsibility, eating white bread, avoiding close relationships, watching telly in bed whenever I liked and basically being accountable to no one. It was an easy life, and I was good at living it.

I never expected to become a stepdad. I didn't see myself falling in love with your mum either, so really if you think about it, all roads lead back to her. She forced me to become a responsible adult when I wasn't ready!

It took me a while to understand the rules of parenting. Still learning. I was good at the easy stuff like going on holiday, theme parks and playing Mario Cart until your fingers went numb. I was great at facilitating lazy mornings with treats and films, spur of the moment days out or trips to the cinema. It was well easy when you were 10 years old. You were never demanding and, even though you'd had some shitty experiences as a kid, you were always up for a laugh and for the first four years I would say we laughed more than anything else.

It's when you became a fully-fledged teenager the wheels began to fall off!

Things got complicated and I could no longer figure out the right thing to do. Then when I did, I couldn't always tell you because you would give us the silent treatment for weeks on end. In many ways, I hated the silence much more than the arguing. It made me feel a bit lost. My man-brain could never find the right words to fix the problem which was very frustrating considering I pride myself on my problem-solving skills, and my ability to step back and analyse a situation.

Obviously not so good when it involves my own decisions.

Plus, it was doubly difficult for my problem-solving brain to compute that the issue was actually mine and not yours. I've had to dig deep to uncover the origin of these issues and I continue to develop my understanding of it all to ensure my reactions are balanced and calm (ish), while dealing with your brothers.

I dread to think what they're going to be like as teenagers!

Yep, it's fair to say we've changed a lot, haven't we? It's been over a decade since we became a family and we've shared the ups and downs, trials, and tribulations of life. I think we've all come out the other side stronger as a family and wiser as individuals.

But getting to this point of understanding has been difficult and I want to say, I'm sorry.

I'm sorry for the times when you've felt like you had nowhere to go. When you didn't feel welcome in your own home. When good days were turned to shit and you were scared of what I might say next or what mood I was in. I'm not suggesting you were an innocent little saint in all of this of course but you deserved my gentler side more often.

I am truly sorry.

But I can't take it back.

I can't say I wish things would've been different because without the drama I wouldn't have learnt so much about myself. Without flushing out so many negative aspects of my personality I wouldn't be the dad I am today, and your brothers wouldn't be benefiting from the person you've helped create.

So, thank you for that. Because you were a flipping walk in the park compared to these two sleep thieves and I can't see how I would've coped with these two ten years ago.

Cold breeze… shudder.

I believe things happen for a reason and you are clearly strong enough to handle almost anything. More than you give yourself credit for I think. Lessons come from the strangest of places sometimes and I'm happy to admit, you've been one of my greatest teachers.

Thank you. I love you. I owe you a drink.

You've had to endure parts of me which were angry and scrambling to control everything, and you've come out the other side of it amazingly.

I'm going to take 40%, minimum, responsibility for your amazingness.

I've always told you things straight. As I see them anyway. Your mum might say sometimes a little too plainly but my openness meant you came to me with issues which you didn't want to discuss with your mum. You've always talked to me about your life or concerns, knowing I wouldn't bullshit you or try and tell you what to do. Exactly. I might have subtly coerced you a few times, but it was always for your own good!

Can I ask, have you forgiven me for the whole Father Christmas debacle or is that still a bit raw? I'm not actually sorry about that. Sorry. I saved you from looking like a right div in secondary school. Believe me.

Anyways, thanks for sticking by me.

Those brothers of yours take so much from your mum and I, as you know, and I truly hope that hasn't made you feel pushed out. That you're not loved equally. Because you are. The great thing is you don't need us like you once did. You're super independent and rocking it on your career path but please know, we are here for you. If you need us, for anything, let us know. Don't think you're so grown up that you can't call us just for a good whinge. Okay?

I love you. I still haven't received that £100 by the way... give me £100!

JACK AND THE BEANSTALK

On reflection, going to the pantomime to watch *Jack and the Beanstalk* on Boxing Day, the day after consuming a years supply of Ferrero Rocher, was probably not the best idea.

'You're going to love it,' said The Wife.
'Oh no I won't.'
'Oh yes you will!'
'Oh no I…'

I was right. It was stressful. Taking small children to any enclosed space where other humans gather sends a cold shiver down my spine at the best of times. Never mind an enclosed space surrounded by likeminded little beasts. All waving around battery powered nunchucks with repeating flashing lights able to produce a hypnotic state a split second before cracking you in the teeth!

'It'll be great. They'll love it.'

My brain can, and often does, replay HD video evidence from the last time, every time, when they've been taken somewhere "They'll love." It always ends the same way, either attempting to manage their behaviour peacefully by talking to them like civil human beings or resorting to bribery. I find it much easier to just pretend they're not mine. Why would this day be any different? Where does The Wife draw her unshakeable faith from?

I'm a realist. I knew exactly how it was going to go.

At the Stockport Plaza on Boxing Day 2019, Ove, then two, was on glorious form. He took it upon himself to act out his own per-formance – one filled with uncontrollable bouts of screaming and contortionism. Each attempt to keep him seated saw every muscle in his little body completely relax and he would flop through my grasp and head under the seats towards the exit. Always towards the exit. Which told me something about how much he was so called loving it. He was like me. We would rather have been at home supping from a bottle of something nice with one hand and stroking our stuffed bellies with the other while watching a film.

Arlo, four at the time and occasionally able to sit still for longer than ten minutes, was enthralled. No bother at all. Unlike his brother. By the half-way point it was obvious we weren't going to make it through the second half in one piece. At times like this when elbowing the popcorn out of the hands of those sitting to my right, blocking the stage from those behind, while passing a tod-dler back and forth between us every minute, I couldn't help but consider if it all would have been better slightly tipsy. But I'd made the, it felt so righteous at the time, suggestion that I wouldn't drink alcohol. Why? Because I'm stupid.

But my brain repeatably forced me to look at the back of the the-atre to the bar where people were getting refreshments before the second half began.

Mind: Go and get a beer.

No.

Mind: You deserve it.

I said I wouldn't.

Mind: You're allowed to change your mind.

Don't say that.

Mind: Look at that dad over there.

I turned to see a fellow dad with two small children who were sitting on either side of him. They were eating chocolate, casually chatting, and waiting patiently while dad sipped on a cold pint. I caught his eye as he dibbed into his super-sized bag of chilli Doritos, washed down with a long gulp from his plastic cup of freezing cold yellow loveliness.

Mind: You want to be that guy.

He's my hero.

I looked beyond that lucky bastard and noticed some empty seats tucked away where the buggies were stored.

We're having those seats!

I immediately sprang into action.

'Where are you going?' The Wife hissed.

Her eyes were watery and wide – she touched my arm and psychically pleaded with me not to leave her alone.

'I have a plan,' I reassured her.

She grasped my wrist so tight I was transported back to primary school when a teacher dragged me along the corridor to the head's office.

'I'll be back in a minute.'

I peeled off one clamped finger at a time then slid out of the cramped seating row like a Ninja towards the Steward who was helping a granny sit down.

'Hi mate. You need to help me. Please.'
'I'll see what I can do.'
'I have two mental kids, one of them may or may not have incarnated in human form to test our physical and mental endurance, but long story short, we need those seats at the back out of the way please.'

He glanced over.

'I'm not sure. It's for wheelchair users.'
'Totally get that, but I've noticed it's not being used today.'
'I'll speak to my supervisor.'

I nodded and stuck to him like glue as he found a grey haired lovely-faced lady stood at an exit, keeping her wise eyes on the crowd. He whispered into her ear and she peered into my soul, recognising a genuine need for help. Plus, I was on my knees with hands clasped together in prayer, shaking them furiously!

She nodded like a pro.

I told her I owed her one and flew down the aisle towards my family. The Wife was holding Ove between her hands as he twisted from side to side and kicked her repeatedly in the chest, like a fish with legs, while spinning the fluorescent front teeth remover above his head.

'Right you three, come on.'

The Wife didn't ask anything. We could've been going home at that point and she wouldn't have argued. She threw both kids through the air one at a time and I placed them against the wall and pinned them there with a foot. The Wife whispered apologies to those collecting teeth off the floor and met me on the aisle.

'What's going on?' she asked.
'Follow me.'

I picked both boys up and walked with purpose past those returning to their seats as the lights were dimmed and the show resumed. The Wife followed, confused, without saying a word. When we arrived at the cordoned off area, the Steward was waiting for us. He removed the rope and waved us to our new private seating area. The kids scrambled out of my arms and immediately got themselves comfy in their own large seats with a clear view of the stage. The Wife hugged the Steward, and I shook his hand vigorously.

The Wife and I made several pleasant sounds as we lowered our battered bodies into the spacious seats. She gave me a look which suggested marrying me was the best thing she'd ever done and if I never accomplished anything else of meaning in my life again, this was enough.

The rest of the show was incident free. Pantomime is not my go-to theatrical form of entertainment, but I appreciate the appeal. It's more relaxed than a regular theatre experience. *Jack and the Beanstalk* was fun, festive, and energised, but the Boxing Day blues seemed to have affected most of the crowd. For a theatrical genre that requires, and greatly benefits from audience participation, my heart went out to the performers. To say the mood was a little flat would be the understatement of the century. I hadn't noticed during the first half because my whole focus was on Ove's escape plans.

It was a tough slog for the performers. Jokes, musical numbers, choreographed routines which might have been enthusiastically applauded on other nights, were met with mild slapping sounds and grunts of interest. Imagine, you've been steadily grazing on pickles, nuts, crisps, and savoury things dipped in cheese all day - you've consumed copious amounts of new and exciting chocolates. You've had your Christmas dinner, probably second helpings and pudding. Maybe some cheese and crackers as well. You honestly can't imagine eating anything else for days.

Then someone asks if you want another mince pie?

No. You didn't have one when you were peckish and tipsy from Bucks Fizz so why would you want one now while bloated and disgusting? You don't. But the inevitable happens. You turn your puffy head ever so slightly to the side and flick an acknowledgment of interest with your forehead while grunting.

That's what the audience response was like.

Even the cheeky scouser playing Simple Simon, who had the best lines and freedom to improvise had to dig deep to drag a response from the lacklustre crowd. I'm not one for public displays of enthusiasm but I felt obliged to raise my game and applaud, jeer, and boooooo in-order to contribute to the show. Whereas in truth, I would usually nod and clap in the right places like a good dad. But not this night. I was right up there with The Wife.

He's behind you.
Oh no he's not.

Booing the bad guy, clapping, laughing loudly, all of it. I honestly didn't think I had it in me.

At the end I looked down at the dad with his empty plastic cup, planning his escape route through the mass of bodies, wild eyed sugar fuelled kids, and neglectful parents slinging baby changing bags over their shoulders. Our eyes met. How quickly roles can be reversed ay mate? I didn't gloat. Didn't have the time because we removed the rope from our VIP area and walked, unmolested, straight out the door and into the crisp December night.

We strolled home with Ove strapped in the buggy while Arlo stood on the buggy board and retold the whole *Jack and the Beanstalk* story to us. The Wife and I nodded and responded cheerily when required. Occasionally we looked into each other's eyes and passed an unspoken word between us as we approached our home.

Wine.

A LOCKDOWN STORY

The longest I've gone without drinking alcohol in the last twenty-four years is two weeks. What's the longest you've ever gone without? Do you even know? It's ingrained into my lifestyle. It's like having a hot drink in the morning. I'm always up for a cold beer or a glass of wine during the week, and once Friday night arrives, if I'm not supping something tasty then I'm either poorly or dead. I can usually slip in another few drinks on Saturday, rough or not, and I love a Sunday afternoon bottle of red while batch cooking for the week.

Reasons to drink:

- Someone dies
- Someone survives
- A baby is born
- Friday night
- Some type of minor achievement
- Batch cooking
- Slightly more stressful day than usual
- Doing the ironing
- No parenting responsibilities for a few hours
- Snotty nose

- Bad mood
- Good mood
- Blue sky

Reasons not to drink:

- Sleeping
- Dead

I'm drinking the less I ever have but I still use alcohol as some type of messed up reward system and essentially, it's kind of dominating my life. But you know what? I'm sick of it. The alcohol consumption doesn't come alone. I smoke roll ups when I drink which I once loved but now find boring. But I can't have one without the other and I'm pretty sure that's called addiction. Plus, I'm susceptible to eating mountains of peanuts, crisps, cheeeeese, lots of cheeeese. Crackers. All the fruit. All the chocolate. All the everything. And in the morning after a night of gorging on red wine and lambs' legs like King Henry the whoever, I've started to feel a bit dirty. Like I've done something wrong. Something shameful. The judgement's not coming from anyone else but myself. But by lunch time I can easily look at a chicken salad and imagine drinking a freezing cold glass of white wine with it. Even if I'm still stinking from the night before.

This relationship with alcohol has been going strong for a long time. I don't know about you, but I started drinking regularly during my first year in secondary school, which was in 1992. And, like many others, I lived in a household where alcohol and socialising were part of life. My Dad's shed was stacked high with bottles of homebrew German lager and wine. There was no way he could keep track of what had been drunk and when, especially after twenty people had been round after the pub listening to records and drinking it. I'd be walking round the lounge handing out bowls of nuts, clearing ashtrays and topping people's glasses up. One for you, one for me. Don't mind if I do. I was caught red handed several times by both parents, but they deemed it acceptable because where else were they going to get that kind of service at 1am on a Saturday night? Nowhere. And *they* weren't going to do it.

It was a similar situation at my Nana's house. My Mum's friends' houses. Everyone smoked. Everyone drank. Even our Babysitters would give me and my brother a glass or two of lager just as long as we didn't give them any jip. It was our reward.

Getting hold of booze when you wanted it was more problematic. You had to endure an evening stood outside a local off license on a Friday night waiting for the right friendly faced adult to come along.

A good Friday night scenario:

'Go in the shop for me, mate?'
'Piss off.'
'Go on.'
'No.'
'Don't be like that.'
'Piss off.'
'I only want a bottle of White Lightening.'

This is a key moment. You stand tall but not confrontational. You've been cheeky and managed to get his attention but now you must somehow show, through a facial expression, that you appreciate the dynamic of the situation. He is in control. He knows it. But he stopped. You're halfway there. In your mind you're screaming, "Come on, come on!" and you reach into your pocket and hold the coins out towards him.

He looks around.

'One bottle?'
'Yeah. White Lightening. A big one.'
'Give it 'ere.'

You try not to get too excited. The transaction is never complete until the cheap plastic bag is in your hand and you're walking towards the safety of the park away from prying adult eyes. You hand over the money. He looks down at the assortment of sweaty coins now in his open palm.

'Shrapnel?'
'I'm fourteen.'
'It'd better be all there.'
'Course it is mate.'

He looks around all sketchy, takes the last blast on his Embassy Number One then flicks it towards the drain. He nods along the road. This is unspoken. You both know the situation. You walk towards the bus stop around the corner. He waits a good fifteen to twenty seconds before entering the shop. The shopkeeper has no clue, but precautions are taken anyway. There's a lot at stake.

Once you arrive at the bus stop you sit and breathe. You visualise.

He goes into the shop, nods at the woman on the stool watching the telly at full volume. He heads over to the fridge, opens the door and takes the large bottle of White Lightening Cider from the bottom shelf. He closes the door then goes to the other fridge with the Stella Artois, he grabs a pack of four, closes the fridge, walks to the counter. "Twenty Number One please." The lady on the stool barely registers his presence, she leans back slightly and takes the cigs from the shelf without looking, chucks them on the counter, punches the prices into the till then rudely asks for the amount shown on the small digital screen on top of the till. He hands her most of my shrapnel and a fresh note. She opens the till, laughs at something on the television. He says, "Can I have a bag please?" NO, NO, NO, what is he doing? She averts her eyes from the TV screen and looks at him as if he's asking for a free foot massage! This could all end badly right now but someone on the show she's watching says something funny again and her boobs jiggle as she laughs. She throws a cheap plastic bag in his

general direction. He packs his beers and my cider into the bag and
says, "Bye," as he leaves the shop.

You open your eyes and he's crossing the road towards the park gates and you follow. He carries the Stella in his hand and passes you the plastic bag as you arrive.

'Here.'
'Nice one, mate. Have a good night yeah,' you say. Buzzing!
'You too.'

He goes one way and you go another. A successful transaction.

An alternative Friday night scenario:

You stand outside in the rain for ages. No one is walking past. You consider giving up, but you endure. Eventually someone comes. They say yes, a little quickly, no hesitation. Your nerves tell you something's off, but you've endured the rain and boredom for about three hours – there's no going back. He takes the money and nods in the direction. Everything appears normal but you know it's not. You wait closer than you usually would and when he exits the shop he walks in the opposite direction. You chase after him and he unceremoniously tells you to "Piss off." And you do because you're fourteen and close to tears. You then commit his face to memory and make plans to punch him several times in the head when you're older and spot him in a nightclub having a great time. You also make a blood vow to buy booze for any kids that ask you when you're old enough because you don't want anyone to go through what you did… but you never do.

The years went by and the booze found many new companions to play with: Amphetamine, Cannabis, LSD, Ecstasy and Cocaine. Those friendships were always just a bit on the side. Alcohol has always been a full-time partnership, a complicated one. Together through thick and thin and all that.

I wrote this many years ago:

I am the shadow in your mind
I create the loss of your time
I am the miss-timed step
I am the promise never kept
I create the blue in your mood
I change the taste of your food
I lend a hand in your hour of need
I decide when it's time to leave
I love you and you love me
We live a life of intimacy
I provide the heat when you are cold
I am every elaborate story ever told
I create the illusion of finesse
I put your moral fibre to the test
I need you and you need me
We share a life of co-dependency
I need your weakness to make me strong
Who were you before I came along?
I gave you courage, power and might
I decide when it's time to fight
You've filled your hole with a liquid soul
I am the reason you lose control
Forever your alcohol

When I wrote that I was also busy with many of the other companions mentioned so it's not a true representation of how I feel
about alcohol now, but it's still a bit grim. The thing is, I don't want
to eliminate alcohol from my life. I just want to take back control
– for Friday to arrive and not automatically think it's time to drink
two bottles of red. To have a proper busy day where I achieve a lot,
and don't congratulate myself by drinking until one eye closes and

I'm eating three crisp butties in a row while standing in the kitchen with only the fridge light for a guide.

So, on Wednesday 30th of September 2020 I had a semi-decent drink which included white wine and vodka tonics. I smoked a few roll ups then chucked the rest in the bin. For the next month I'm off the drink. The cigs are gone. Come November with so much spare time on my hands I expect to be fluent in Spanish, look ten years younger, have a passive income from a brand-new business venture which takes the world by storm. To have sanded down the filler in the bathroom walls which has been there for yonks, and hopefully found a fruit tea which doesn't make me want to puke. Here's to making it longer than two weeks. Cheers.

(I lasted 29 days then moved to a new house with my family and celebrated with some beers. You know, as a reward!)

THEY WIN

They win. They've finally won. They're the champions. They've won the battle and the war. We've been beaten so mercilessly I honestly don't know why we didn't wave the white flag years ago. Life could've been soooo much easier if we had done.

Congratulations you little sleep thieves!

I don't even feel bad about it. I'm glad they've won. They've put so much effort into playing the game it would've been a pity for them to lose in the end. The only real shame is they have no idea they were even playing in the first place.

At least they can't be smug about it.

It's all so clear now, here at the end. Defeated. Relieved. I can look back at all the pain and suffering of war, the fatigued bodies limping towards the kitchen for the tenth cup of tea before 10am, dressed in dirty (un-ironed) rags, red eyed and unable to remember which white box was for dishes and which one was for rags, and I see how pointless it all was.

That's the painful bit – hindsight – looking back at what could have been if we'd only understood we were fighting a losing battle.

Actually, I do feel bad.

Bad for The Wife and I who've been participating in a war we were ill-equipped to fight!

Many moons ago, when I could venture out after dark wearing nice clothes and aftershave, I played poker at a pub. I'd never really played before, but I had a general idea what to do. *Real* poker players, people who have invested time and energy into their craft, hate playing against people like me. I wasn't following a strategy or thinking about the other person's hand. I was working off Guinness, luck and a naïve intuition about my own hand which worked amazingly and got me a seat in the final; where it all unravelled terribly because I was eight pints in and thinking more about the jukebox than the game. But was I bothered? Not at all. I'd knocked several well-seasoned players out the game and I didn't really know how I was doing it.

'Two pairs, Kings and Jacks,' Seasoned Player said.

He placed his cards on the table. Chuffed.

'Argh, you got me,' I said. 'Two pairs as well but I only have tens. I was close though.'

His knuckles turned white.

'You have a Full House.'
'Is that good?' I enquired.

I think he went straight home to bed.

You see, they were stressing and getting annoyed, and I was just enjoying myself, drinking Guinness, munching crisps, going for a smoke, and playing my favourite tunes on the jukebox. It was a great night. There was nothing these experienced players could do to stop me because, like my boys, I wasn't emotionally connected to the outcome. I was just living my life, placing cards on a table, and hoping for the best. The outcome didn't really matter because I was enjoying all the aspects of the evening.

Now I know how it must have felt for them; to be playing against an ignorant person (and I mean that in its truest sense, a person with a lack of knowledge) and think you can somehow come out on top just because you have more experience - because you have *the knowledge.* Ha. It doesn't always work out like that I'm afraid because when you're playing against two agenda-less sleep thieves your past experiences aren't worth a damn.

My boys won. They cleared up. Royal flush!

The Wife and I now go to bed at 8pm.

At the latest. Earlier most days.

Do you remember being a kid and complaining to your parents about going to bed while it was still sunny outside? I'm not going to do that because we accept that we will not sleep, ever again, past 5am. Bed for 8pm with the very real chance of getting to sleep for 9pm which actually gives us eight, mainly undisturbed, hours' sleep. The best we've had it in six years. Why am I not thrilled with this prospect? I should be buzzing! I'll tell you why I'm not. It's a well-known fact that nothing exciting, in the whole of human history, has ever happened to people who go to bed before 8pm.

Nothing… Ever!

It never has and never will.

Well, maybe one small thing? Going to bed earlier means it's acceptable to open a bottle of wine earlier. 4pm to be exact. This means wine with tea which I've been advocating for ages. The Wife has been strictly against it, since the whole brush with alcoholism fiasco during the first lockdown, and because putting the kids to bed after consuming wine makes her sleepy. She still sits with them until they fall asleep. Cute. Me? I take the boys to bed, speed read through two books, kiss them both, turn the light off, say good-night, and shut the door. Job done in fifteen minutes whereas it once took hours. So you know what? I was feeling defeated but it's clear now we're all winners here. This is a shared victory. Going to bed at 8pm is cool and I'm very happy about it.

Did that sound convincing to you? I almost believed it myself

BEING DAD

He thinks it's an identity crisis. Sort of. Although the word crisis doesn't fit because he likes it. It feels good. He was so sure of who he was and what he liked once but now the memory of that guy is rapidly fading. He gets caught off guard. He might be brushing his teeth, opening a bottle of wine, lying in the dark hoping that was the cat who just thudded in the other room at four am, and not one of his boys getting up. In those off-guard moments, a not so exciting image from the past POPS into his mind's eye suddenly. He watches it, confused, "Why is my brain showing me this?" then continues to observe as it develops into a little movie in his head where he's cooking spaghetti bolognaise in a grubby kitchen where he lived years ago. He even had hair!

An all-knowing sense of what else happened on that utterly normal evening will merge with the movie in his head. The music playing - he can't hear it but knows it's there - is probably one of the mixed CD's he used to make regularly. He's swigging red wine from a half pint glass. How uncouth. He's halfway through the first bottle, and a second will be finished; one was never enough. He'll smoke a couple of roll ups like he always did when having a drink and, without fail, he'll spend most of the evening watching films and texting several different female acquaintants. Social media hadn't taken over back then. Simpler days.

That young man was passionate about things. Full of energy, anger, and love! There was a fire in his belly that pushed him to get things done without over complicating the idea. He knows the image of the young man is from his twenties and rationally he's aware of the traits of a young man at that age, but why this image? Why now? Is he supposed to acknowledge that there's a part of himself which has gone and will never return? Has the fire gone? Did it burn out or was it taken away?

Now life needs a plan. He can't just have an idea and pursue it 24/7 until satisfied. Passion has been replaced with a dream board filled with images, dates, and cheesy motivational phrases.

"A dream is just a goal without a plan." "Be your authentic self." "You're worthy of success."

He looks at that dusty dream board. How did he get to the point where pursuing an idea needed visualising on a piece of card? Gradually he began replacing his hobbies, wants, passions, dreams, youth, desires, friendships, social life, career, all day drink and drug sessions, gigs, doing fack all, personal hygiene, personal development, putting sugar in tea, eating microwave pizza and chips, watching all three *Lord of the Rings* special edition boxsets in bed just because he had a hint of a cold, with the wants and needs of his family.

Is that just the way it goes? Does it have to be like that?

All those things are now a series of blended images in his mind that no longer fit coherently together. Like a damaged jigsaw. Some of the pieces have been chewed around the edges. They're soggy. Others have faded. He can look at the image on a piece and know what it's supposed to be – he can see a person who looks like him standing with some other people, who he kind of recognises, in a place he's sure he's been, but he just can't place himself there anymore. It's just floating around in the jigsaw of his mind, existing but without a place. No context.

After experiencing all this madness in his mind, he returns to the present with another word in mind, gratitude. He wouldn't be anywhere else in the world if you paid him. He doesn't want to be that guy cooking in the kitchen alone. His life was hard. Full of unexpected challenges which occasionally broke him and left him deflated. Everything was fought hard for and easily lost. The desire to live at a hundred miles per hour, jam packing in as many sensory experiences as possible, has matured into a quality over quantity kind of attitude. Watching his boys live their lives gives him a much deeper pleasure than he knew possible. Sharing a bottle of wine with his wife, allowing her to win at cards while discussing their present, is significantly more satisfying than the fly-by-night relationships from the past.

If the only two jobs he did well in this life were being a good dad and a loving husband, he'd be happy with that. And grateful for the opportunity.

Mums of the World, I Get it Now!

It's hard work being a parent, someone should be paying us to do it. I'm not joking. Without the kids of the now, who'll be the adults of the future? And if our sleep deprived brains finally slide out of the dish, who's going to care for them? I have a vision of social services knocking on the door.

'Hello, Mr Glennon, we've come to check on you and partner. We've had reports your children are attempting to push you into a catatonic state?'
'Yhnnsn beeeeeee.'
'Yes, milk and two sugars please.'
'Hhgeee beeeeya.'
'Soya milk's fine.'

I wave her inside and she follows me into the lounge where the children are hanging upside down from rope swings attached to the ceiling. They're both naked and filthy. Smeared with the remnants of food and messy play. Wide eyed and alert. Chewing slowly on something fruit-like and sticky. The Wife's sitting at the table facing the window.

'Mmnnhxh knjcsnsjj.'
'Okay, Babe,' The Wife says without turning.

I go off to the kitchen to make the brews.

'How long's he been talking like that?'
'Three weeks now. I couldn't understand him at first. I had to, tune in.'
'It's very common in new Dads. Especially ones who survived the nineteen nineties. They don't have many brain cells left to begin with and parenthood, well, it can easily take the rest.'
'Taggy waggy woooo… ahem. Sorry.'

The Wife wraps her arms tightly around herself and begins to rock gently.

'I can see you're in the very early stages too, Mrs Glennon. How long's it been happening?'
'This morning at 04:52am when the boys decided it was time to turn their bedroom into a den. They needed all our covers and cushions apparently. I think I was trying to say get out of our room but instead I blurted out, "Taggy waggy woooo."'
'Does Mr Glennon know?'

The Wife laughs hysterically. Her head swings wildly from side to side. She stamps her feet against the laminate floor.

'Mrs Glennon?'

The Wife stops instantly.

'Does Mr Glennon know, you ask?'

I step into the lounge with a large tray which I place on the dining table next to The Wife. The social worker steps forward and gasps in horror but recovers her composure quickly. I pass a miniature Sylvanian Family teacup to The Wife and one to the social worker who accepts it with great care as if it contains a hot liquid. She even gives it a little blow.

'Thanks.'
'Taggy waggy woooo,' I tell her.

The Wife turns in her chair.

'Taggy waggy wooo,' The Wife says.
'Taggy waggy wooo,' both the boys say.

They drop to the floor, landing directly on their heads, then get up, completely unaffected, and begin walking slowly towards the social worker. They continue ripping large chunks from an unidentified red fruit. The social worker places the miniature teacup back on the tray and begins a slow but purposeful retreat towards the hall-way and eventual freedom.

'Someone from my office will be in touch,' she says before gently closing the front door behind her.

We all stand at the window and wave her off whilst sipping from our miniature teacups.

I think £30,000 per year to be a parent sounds about fair. I've had numerous jobs throughout my life, and none are as demanding as being a domesticated stay-at-home dad. And to all the mums who have been doing it from day one, you deserve some kind of back payment. A damages cheque in the post. Recognition for services to humanity or something.

To all the mums, I salute you. And apologise on behalf of all the unappreciative kids and husbands out there. We didn't know!

We didn't know you had to put in a wash *every* day. That not all items of clothing can go in the dryer. We didn't know there wasn't a magical way to pair socks or get the creases out of jeans without ironing them. It never occurred to us you might want some time off for yourself. We thought you liked doing everything. We just didn't know. We couldn't see past our own needs. Again, I'm sorry.

But I know now, oh how I know now!

I've broken through the veil of ignorance. I see you now. I know your pain. We're in this together. When I see the occasional parent outside nursery in the morning, smartly dressed, fresh faced and composed, I think, who are these freaks of nature? What's their secret? I want to tug at their sleeve, whisper into their ear, "How do you do it? You look so *clean*." But as the urge to speak merges with my ability to register the idea, I realise I'm standing with the car fob in my hand staring at an old man in the reflection of the car window. He resembles me, slightly. I swear I recognise those tired red eyes but there's an unidentified brown smear on his left cheek and he looks broken – close to tears. How many days straight as he worn that t-shirt? Does he know it's tucked into his back-to-front boxer shorts?

Is that really me?

I'm going to go out on a limb and say out right that some parents have it harder than others but if you've been away for the weekend without your kids while they're still under three, you guys don't have a flipping clue.

I used to smile a lot, wear skinny jeans, and a variety of funky look-ing shoes. Now I live in shorts and hoodies, splattered with por-ridge and jam, but at least it's organic, ha, ha, ha, ha, ha, sniffle, sniffle, sob, sob. Seriously how did it come to this? The kids are always poorly, and they don't sleep. When I hear a parent say, "Oh, little Joshy had me up all night, he didn't go to sleep till 8pm and woke up at 6am, I'm exhausted." My eye twitches and I want to grab that parent by the shoulders and shake them violently while screaming in their face, "You have no idea!" before falling at their feet sobbing, begging them to let me sleep at their house for a night.

At its worst, when Arlo was a baby, he would sleep for fifty minutes and scream for twenty. That was almost every night for two and a half years before he was diagnosed with glue ear. It nearly broke us. Now, he only wakes once or twice a night. Manageable. Ove however, one year old, also suffering with glue ear, wakes about six times a night but he only cries and doesn't scream, ha, ha, ha, ha, ha, sniffle, sniffle, sob, sob. Seriously how did it come to this?

I know we aren't the only ones suffering with this job. I see those freaks of nature parents looking fresh faced and organised, and I know it's fakery. They've probably had a couple of good days on the bounce and they've got a bit giddy and bothered to shower. I mainly meet the *other* parents, the ones like me; the confused, the lethargic. They walk the supermarket aisles with upside down shopping lists looking for foods they would never have bought five years ago. We walk past one another, a knowing look is exchanged, words aren't necessary. We both know what this day is. Nursery day! I adjust the shopping list for her, and she wipes the crumbs from my shoulder. We force a smile and continue along our way.

We should be paid for this job!

"No one asked you to have kids," I hear some of you say.

That's not true. The Wife did.

When calculating our financial worth as a parent: Combine our daily cleaning chores, dealing with the tricksy washing basket (which makes you question reality because it's impossible to empty completely) with the constant detective work required to locate all the discarded food and spiky toys on the floor. Add childcare, medical services, emotional support, human punchbag and hourly comedic performances and I'm sure we'd be worth £60,000 per year but I'm a realist. I'd happily settle for £30,000 to develop two compassionate, empathic adults of the future. What do you think, are we worth it? Ya damn right!

TO MY BOYS

Hello Boys. I really hope I'm not in a mental institute while you're reading these words but anything's possible. I could be dead! If that's the case make sure your mum has erected a shrine to my greatness somewhere in the house. It doesn't have to be the front room. I'd be happy with the kitchen where I've spent most of my life since your mum decided she can only make jacket potato and beans.

But it's unlikely I've met with an untimely demise because despite your best efforts to cripple us both mentally through a relentless, and I mean this Boys, your *relentless* attack on our basic human right to sleep longer than four hours, I'm in pretty good shape. Your Mum? She's currently walking around in circles looking for her sanity after a particularly early rise of 04:50am by you Ove G. She's got to get ready for work soon and attempt to act normal for the day. I don't know how she does it. You two have no idea. We protect you from the despair by pushing through and finding a way to cope. I'm currently researching the legality of placing bolts on both of your doors because I'm a doer!

It's lucky you're both cute.

Ove, you recently turned three. You are obsessed with toy fighting and weapons. I have a cut on my head where you cracked me on the head with a wooden sword yesterday. Fanks. You also love lying down twiddling our nipples to the point of scabbing while sipping on a fine oat milk. You're still finding your voice but the language you've created is beautiful and we understand most of it. Lockdown March 2020 came at a key stage in your personal development. This was prime learning and socialising time and unfortunately it took those opportunities away from you. But you're very happy and we're trying our best to support you the best we can while you figure out what you like to do and what your interests are.

Arlo, you're, in your own words, five and a half and three quarters. You love making up stories and songs which you soothe Ove with, in the middle of the night, after I've plonked him back in his own bed. Your stories are fantastical and funny. You merge your personal experiences with other stories and songs you've heard with great skill. You're a very gentle person who loves being around other people. You regularly congratulate strangers for their choice in hair colour, fashion sense, or anything else that springs to your mind. This always brings a smile to even the grumpiest of faces.

You bring so much laughter into the world Boys and I'm 100% accurate in saying this, you get your humour from me. Ha-ha Wife, write your own book.

Oh, but you both love a good kick off too. Snacks and technology are the source of most of these eruptions. There're several ways we manage this. Good old-fashioned "no." Your mum's favourite. I tend to lean on the classics like hide and seek or other physical games because, fundamentally, you both love playing more than anything else. You just don't know that yet. Sometimes, me and your mum are too tired to play because, read the rest of the book to find out all the details, but sleep deprivation has pushed us to the very limit of human endurance and every so often all we have to offer is our unconditional love, chocolate, and bubbles.

But the crazy thing is I wouldn't change anything. Life is what it is Boys. Living with two sleep thieves has also pushed us towards positive things: Self-development, reflection, endurance, and love. The desire to relinquish old wounds and behaviours underpinned by our own traumas which laid the groundwork for our personalities, fears, quirks, biases, addictions, anger management skills, or lack of, etc etc etc!

Basically, I won't apologise for snapping now and again and you don't have to apologise for nearly killing us through sleep deprivation. Deal? Cool.

Things have changed a lot.

It's just the four of us now since moving to Plymouth, leaving Becca behind in Stockport. That was a huge decision. Not one we ever expected to make. A proper fork in the road moment for us all. It came down to several factors and one being she didn't need us as much as she once did. She's a young woman now and we wouldn't have entertained the idea of moving unless we believed 100% in Becca's ability to handle it. Probably 80-85% to be honest. It's tough sometimes because we don't have anyone else here with us. We're still trying to utilise video calls to Granny and Grandpa, and Nana and Grandad. It's not the same of course and we know that. But it was part of the sacrifice we had to make because we were, and continue to be, convinced that it was important to offer you both something different. We want you to have experiences that we never had.

This wasn't a completely selfless act. We wanted new and exciting opportunities for ourselves as well. But this period of our lives is also filled with external challenges that are preventing us from having a well-balanced mixture of experiences that humans deserve to have. We disapprove with the lockdowns in all forms but here in our home, we focus on the positives Boys and we shield ourselves from the fear-based media which portrays a bleak existence for us all when in truth, this world is pretty amazing and most of the people you'll meet are as well.

In my emerging view people must elevate themselves above fear and look inside. Feel their emotions and heal their psychological wounds. And outwardly it would be helpful if the world got rid of the elite ruling class, human trafficking, carcinogens from the food and water, glitter, hourly news updates on the radio, porn's probably got to go. Having loads of different device chargers is an absolute waste of time. Updating software is another. World hunger has always been a problem. How's it looking now? Has amazing technology changed everything for the better? Or has AI enslaved humans and forced us all to live as one nation? No more wars or borders? Healthy living and no recreational drugs? A perfect balance of work, rest, and obedience? Sounds a bit boring to me.

Life is risk Boys and sometimes you get hurt.

Your mum and I can't control those things, so we concentrate on being the best we can be. When you read this for the first time, hopefully, we're still fully alive and kicking, and working hard together to give you and ourselves the best life we can.

But seriously, technology is an issue. Arlo, you like to ask, "Can I have my iPad," until you've bombarded my subconscious so profoundly, I begin to think it's my idea and give in. Arlo, just so you know, it's an Amazon Fire Tablet, not an iPad. Ove G, you like to rock in from nursery and point and scream at the telly until I put it on. I can dissuade you for a few minutes with a snack, you're just getting into puzzles, or by chasing you around the house like a mad man for a few minutes but all roads lead back to finger pointing and screaming at the telly.

Just so you know, we're gathering our strength Boys and the winds of change are coming!

A combination of lockdown restrictions and the winter weather have contributed towards more time indoors and an overreliance on devices. But spring is in the air and I'm hopeful for the lighter days ahead. Technology has its place but there must be a way to introduce a healthy balance between screen time and play time. When I was young computers were in their infancy. The options on the telly were limited and you pretty much had to watch whatever the oldest person in the room wanted to. You boys get a lot of freedom and I just want you both to know now, if the screaming and shouting continues, I will sell every device in the house and move us into a caravan.

Maybe you're reading this now from that caravan with a mullet haircut and dodgy teeth?

Here's in the inside scoop Boys: We don't know what we're doing! It's tough. As adults we juggle much more than you know. Everything is free for you both and it's our job, the best job in the world, to make sure you have the things you need, within reason, and you feel loved and secure. I think we do a pretty good job at that. Any complaints? Take it up with your mother.

At the minute Ove, you won't even entertain the thought of riding your little blue balance bike. When you didn't have one, all you wanted to do was try and have a go on other children's bikes. Now you have your own, do you care? Not at all. And that's fine son. We are here to facilitate your interests as long as it's not eating pebbles or nipple twiddling. I hope you can ride your bike because I know it's lots of fun but maybe it's not like that for you right now. Maybe you feel out of control? If I had to choose between swimming and riding a bike though, I'll take swimming any day, Son. That's a natural life skill we all should acquire. You can't cycle away from a jellyfish.

It's tough for you at the moment Arlo because you're not getting a lot of time for independent play at home. Yes, we run around the house inventing games and setting traps but finding some alone time with your own thoughts has become more difficult. And that difficulty is also your best friend. Ove G. Just when you've set everything up, world building with blocks to the left, and a battered selection of cars scattered to the right, Ove G comes along and destroys it! It's 100% his favourite thing to do. We can't stop him, Son. He's relentless in his quest to destroy your independent play. Sorry about that. But if it makes you feel any better, just know you're his favourite person in the world and he loves you incredibly.

This book is basically dedicated to you. Without documenting our experiences, in a way which hopefully brings a smile to people's faces, I would never had learnt so much about myself and my potential as a parent. So nice one. Thanks. But I want you to know that very soon your mum and I will be going away for a long weekend, and guess what... four's a crowd. Not sure how it's going to manifest yet, but I see cold drinks in the evening sun. Beautiful sea views. Quiet time. Holding your mum's hand as we smile at one another, knowing you two lovely boys are sleeping somewhere familiar with people that love you. Or at least like you enough to let you sleep over. I'm not going to lie; we aren't as fussy as we used to be.

Anyway... thank you Arlo and Ove. Thanks for teaching me so much about myself. Thanks for bringing us so much joy and love. Thanks for all of it. And if by any chance I do find my way into a mental institute, tell them I like the trippy drugs. Stronger the better.

Cheers Boys.

Printed in Great Britain
by Amazon

63484653R00131